creating
moments
of
JOY

for the Person with Alzheimer's or Dementia

by
Jolene Brackey

Editors: Helene Bergren, Dave DeValois
Cover Design: Alison Shepard

4th Edition

Enhanced Moments
email: jolene@enhancedmoments.com
www.enhancedmoments.com

04   03   02   5   4   3

∞ The paper used in this book meets the minimum requirements of
American National Standards for Information Sciences—Permanence
of Paper for Printed Library Materials, ANSI Z39.48-1992.

Printed in the United States of America.

I would like to gratefully acknowledge all of the writers who I have quoted for their
wisdom and inspirational words. If there is an error concerning permission to reprint, I
apologize and a correction will be made in subsequent editions.

Library of Congress Cataloging-in-Publication Data
Brackey, Jolene Anne
        Creating moments of joy / Jolene Brackey
             p.   cm.
Includes bibliographical references.
ISBN 1-55753-366-0
        1. Alzheimer's disease—Patients—Care—Psychological aspects.
2. Alzheimer's disease—Patients—Home care—Psychological aspects.
3. Dementia—Patients—Care—Psychological aspects. 4. Dementia—
Patients—Home care—Psychological aspects. I. Title
RC523.2 B73 2004
362.1'9683

ACKNOWLEDGEMENTS

To the people with Alzheimer's disease—for giving me treasures for a lifetime.

To the CNAs and Activity Directors—for passing on all your wonderful ideas. You have "it."

To Deb—for being my guiding light.

To my close friends—for believing in me and giving me fond memories filled with joy.

To Ron Kitterman—for your understanding of spiritual well-being. It is the glue that holds my words together.

To Lori—for your words of wisdom and encouragement.

To Julie, Paula, Dave and Helene—for not only editing my book, but feeling my emotions.

To Heidi—for patiently offering insights on how to "wrap" up my thoughts.

To Terry—for capturing my thoughts into drawings.

To David—for the opportunity to fulfill my dreams.

To Renae—for patiently and diligently putting up with me.

To Teresa—for sharing this adventure with me.

To my family—together we are a foundation as solid as a rock.

To Troy, Sidney, Taylor and Keegan—You are my treasures!

To my mom and dad–
for your love,
faithfulness and
for giving me
wings to fly.

This journal belongs to

who lives at

I, _____,

am the primary care person and I live at

my phone number is: (   )

*If you want to know more about us, just look inside
this book. You will open the window to our hearts.*

Create a Moment of Joy!

CONTENTS

Memory Enhanced Environments

Enhanced Moments

How to Use This Journal

I have a vision. A vision that we will soon look beyond the challenges of Alzheimer's disease and focus more of our energy on *creating moments of joy.* When a person has short-term memory loss, his life is made up of moments. We are not able to create a perfectly wonderful day with those who have dementia, but it is absolutely attainable to create perfectly wonderful moments—moments that put smiles on their faces, a twinkle in their eyes, or trigger memories. Five minutes later, they won't remember what you did or said, but the feeling you left them with will linger.

I have broken down the learning process into five sections. Within those sections are smaller steps. At the end of each step is a place where you can journal your thoughts, solutions, and treasures to help you achieve the overall goal of creating many moments of joy for the person with dementia, and for YOU!

Understand the person with Alzheimer's – This is your foundation. You need to understand where the person believes he is living in his mind before you can respond with acceptance and patience.

Powerful Tools That Create Positive Outcomes – Here's where you begin to understand what people with dementia are communicating through their daily patterns of actions and words.

Let's Talk Communication – Learn more about your loved ones by changing the way you communicate. Once you find the treasures they hold, you will enhance their lives by reminding them who they are.

Memory Enhanced Environments – In this section, you will discover what triggers a sense of comfort in their surroundings. When they are comfortable, they will find peace in their environment.

Enhanced Moments – Discover what will bring back joy to the person, and to YOU!

If you take just one thing with you after reading this book, I hope you gain the courage to try everything once.

You will make mistakes. Mistakes are treasures too, because they teach you what not to do. As long as you keep trying, you and your loved one still have hope. When you find the treasure, write it down and practice, practice, practice. Let go of all your expectations. Savor the simple surprises you receive along the way.

Scribble notes everywhere about anything at all, so wants and wishes are not lost, but are bound together in this personal journal. When the time comes, pass on this journal filled with your solutions and treasures.

It is also my true desire to create moments of joy for you, the person who holds and reads this book. I have carefully selected stories, quotes, and dashes of humor—hoping that you will remember, cry, laugh, and love.

When we learn with pleasure, we never forget.
— Alfred Mercier

— *Prelude* —

*Bob was an avid fly fisherman, and loved fishing the
streams of Oregon. I met Bob when he moved into our
community after being diagnosed with Alzheimer's.
He had a wonderful relationship with his wife. I asked
her to bring me one of Bob's fishing poles. We were all
outside enjoying the sun when his wife opened the door
with a fishing pole in her hand. I gave the pole to Bob
and asked if he would show us how to cast. He tossed
the line out with such ease—and then handed me the
fishing pole. Needless to say, I didn't do very well, but
he enjoyed watching me try. Then I asked him, "How
do you tie the lures on?" He grabbed into the air for a
fishing line, which wasn't really there, and he moved
his hands and fingers as if he were tying the knot. He
looked over at me with the imaginary knot in his hand
and a smile on his face. I said, "You're amazing." And
he just laughed.*

This is what I mean by "creating a moment of
joy." Bob relived one of his own simple pleasures,
fly fishing. A pastime he loved. If his wife had not
brought in his fishing pole, this moment would not have
occurred. We would have missed our opportunity to
create a moment of joy, but instead we captured it.
We created a moment of joy for the people who lived
there, a moment of joy for me, for his wife, and most
importantly, a moment of joy for him.

Understanding the Person with Alzheimer's

Understand that a person with Alzheimer's will lose his short-term memory, but retain some long term memory if we learn how to trigger it. The first part of the brain that is damaged affects the short-term memory. This is why they repeat their stories, why they cannot remember what they had for breakfast or that their son visited last night. When you ask them what they had for breakfast they say, "I didn't have breakfast. Would you make me some?" Switch to their long-term memory and ask what they like to eat for breakfast, cereal or pancakes? They can chat about what they like to eat, but they cannot chat about what they just ate.

When you say to them, "I heard your son came to visit you last night." The response goes like this, "I haven't seen him in months. Where is my son?" Again, switch to their long-term memory, "He is such a wonderful kid, and he has big brown eyes just like you. You must be a proud mama." We can give her her son back . . . not from last night, but we can remind her who he is.

16

During a discussion about pets, Tom piped up about his pet mule. He said, "I had a pet mule once named Topsie. The only way to get Topsie to work for me was to share my tobacco with him." I asked him how old he was, and he said, "I was about 15 or 16." Tom is 82 years old, and doesn't remember what he had for breakfast, but he still remembers details from his childhood. He not only remembered how old he was and the name of his mule, but he remembered how to get Topsie to work for him. That's a treasure!

Because of the their short term memory loss they will share the same story over and over again. The following story is a true example of this.

I love to walk in the rain. As I was walking by the care center I thought, "I am going to go in and create a moment of joy." It never fails, the people there always create one for me. My hair was soaked and the ladies wanted to get me a towel. I explained how I loved the water. I am a lifeguard; I love to swim and walk in the rain. One of the ladies told me how she was a good swimmer, too, and taught all of her children to swim. She also told me about when she was eight and there were two kids in the river. They weren't very old and didn't look like they were going to make it. So she swam out and grabbed the girl by the hair and told the boy he better hang on. She wasn't very big and about the time when she didn't know if she would make it, she touched bottom and pushed the kids to shore with all her strength. I said, "Wow, you saved their lives." She said, "All I know is, I was shaking and I didn't swim for two years after that."

Now guess how many times I heard that story in the 15 minutes I visited with her....five times. My wet hair triggered her story over and over again. Now, you can look at the stories they repeat over and over and over again and think, "Ahh, I already heard that story 10 times." Or you can look at that story and think, "I better remember this story for him because his disease might progress and he might lose the ability to tell me his story." When that time comes, the story that may put a smile on their face is the one that irritated you. These things that irritate you today might become treasures tomorrow.

Two months later, I visited this lady again and just said, "Hey, ya been swimming lately?" She replied, "No, but when I was eight...." And she proceeded to tell me the whole story again. All I had to say was the word "swimming." At that point I wished everyone knew the word "swimming," and I wished people would come up to her all day long and ask, "Hey, ya been swimming lately?" Then she would get to tell her story over and over and over again. Do you not think she would get a better day? Absolutely! Because the story leaves her with a good feeling.

Everything is in the process of being forgotten. But who we are—who we have been in mood, in personality, in character—persists much longer

—David Dodson Gray

As the Disease Progresses, Age Regresses

As the disease progresses, a person with Alzheimer's gets younger and younger and younger in his mind. In other words, early in the disease they may have only lost the last 20 years, but as the disease progresses they may lose the last 40 years, the last 60 years, and so on. This is why they don't recognize their spouses, because in their mind, they think they are 25 and their spouses are too old because they have grey hair. They also may ask where their moms are, or get up and want to go to school.

If they begin talking to the mirror, they are really talking to another person because they don't recognize themselves. That person in the mirror is much older than they are. Talking to a mirror usually has a negative effect because the person in the mirror doesn't talk back or may look ill. If they are having negative reactions, then remove the mirror. But if they are having a lovely conversation with the person in the mirror, it is a good thing. Pay close attention to their facial expressions. They will tell all.

People with Alzheimer's even revert back to their native language. If a person lived in Germany until she was 15, she might start talking German again. If you no longer understand what she is saying, determine if she is talking in her native tongue. Then try to learn some words in her native language.

How do you figure out what age they are living? The simplest way is to ask them, "How old are you?" If they do not respond or show confusion answering this question, there are other ways to figure it out. If a man is looking for his spouse, but does not recognize her, you can assume he remembers they are married—which is usually between the age of 20 to 40. If a woman is looking for her children and does not recognize them, you can assume they are in younger adulthood—perhaps twenties or thirties. If they are looking for their parents, you can assume they are in adolescence. Once you figure out what age they are living, then figure out what was significant in their life at that time. Use that information to create moments of joy.

I heard a story about a gentleman who angrily walked around yelling, "Horse! Horse!" Staff labeled him as agitated and usually avoided him because his yelling was so annoying. They eventually decided to talk to the family about this "behavior." The family replied that when he was in his 20s, he took care of horses. With this understanding, they brought in a saddle, reins, cleaning supplies and pictures of horses and filled his room with items familiar to him. His yelling diminished, and he would clean the saddle and reins for long periods of time.

It's exciting!! Once we understand why these great people we care for do what they do, then we accept the challenges with a positive outlook. We now have energy to find a solution instead of dwelling on the problem. Behaviors, or more positively called actions and reactions are windows to a person's mind, and we can help bring light to that window.

Our value lies in what we are and what we have been, not in our ability to recite the recent past.
—Homer, a man with Alzheimer's disease

Newfound Understanding

understanding the person with alzheimer's

"Not Forgotten"

We need to clarify a thought we have, a comment we might make to others. It has to do with your loved one's ability to know who he or she is seeing when he or she sees you right now, how you are today. This person may not recognize you, but he or she has not forgotten you. When we say, "They won't remember you," we are giving a hopeless message. Alzheimer's is not hopeless. You need to understand she may not *recognize* you, because she thinks of you as a child, or as a young handsome husband. I assure you they have not forgotten you.

> This gentleman's name was Bud and his wife has Alzheimer's. He decided to take his wife to the park where they used to go parking as teenagers. He leaned over, touched her cheek, and said, "I love you." She said, "I'm sorry sir, but my heart is for Bud." Now, he could look at the negative side and think, "She doesn't know me." Or he could look at the positive side and say with a smile, "She still loves ME!!!!!!"

Children with parents who have Alzheimer's: it's important to know they have not forgotten you.

A friend of mine has a mother with Alzheimer's. And my friend wished much for her mom just to say her name, Virginia. She wanted to know that her mom remembered her. During a care conference, a staff person told her that her mom carries around a doll whom she calls Virginia. This was the ultimate gift—to know her mom was holding her!!

The other fascinating discovery is they don't forget a tone of voice. They will recognize your voice far into the disease, but you have to get out of their sight in order for this to happen.

A son went to visit his mom and walking down the hall he called "Mom!" She replied, "Larry! Larry!" But as soon as the son was close enough for her to see, she didn't know who he was.

A sister would visit her brother. During the visit she would stand behind him rubbing his back and giving him memories from their childhood. They would have pretty good conversation. But as soon as she came around the front and he saw her face, the wall would go up, and he would be confused.

Now I would like you to imagine another situation that happens frequently. The lady has Alzheimer's and she is in her own home where her husband is taking care of her. She is sitting in her chair and looks over and sees a strange man in her house. How will that make her feel at that moment? Scared? When is he going to leave? So then she scurries out of the house and goes to the neighbors house to call 911 because there is a man in her house.

Now I would like you to imagine how the husband feels when he has been married to this lady for 50 years, and now his wife is frightened of him. When he tries to care for her, she hits him and cusses at him. How does he feel? Horrible, if he doesn't understand Alzheimer's. Let me share a story from a husband who was very creative when his wife was looking for him but didn't recognize him.

When my wife would ask for me and I knew she didn't recognize me. I would go outside and stand for about 5 minutes, and then I would come through front door with my familiar, "Honey, I'm home. I'm going to the garage for a minute." As long as my wife didn't see my face it worked because she recognized my voice, and thought I was home.

—Husband

Turn this around and imagine the husband with Alzheimer's and his wife is taking care of him. He is sitting in his house. He looks over and sees this older lady with an apron on. First thought, "There will be good food for supper." Smile. People with dementia only know what they see right now. Who has grey hair and an apron? Grandma. Who do we feel safe with? Grandma. Who makes good food? Grandma. In most situations it is much more difficult for a man to be caregiver for his wife, because she doesn't feel safe with this strange man.

One more scenario that is a bit more painful. A daughter shared with me how when she visits her mom, her mom just swears at her and tells her to get out of her house. So the daughter and her dad must visit in another room. Through the tears, I imagined what the person with dementia was seeing, because they only know what they see right now. The mom doesn't recognize her daughter because her daughter, in her mind, is a little girl. So this woman coming in the house and going into another room with her husband is "the other woman." If the daughter never understands why her mom yells at her and tells her to get out, this response will happen over and over again. How do you think the daughter will eventually feel about her mom? BUT if the daughter understood what her mom was seeing she may realize a better way to visit would be to bring flowers to her mom with a note from her dad saying, "I love you." Then, visiting with mom—as if she was a friend or neighbor or the flower delivery person.

Daughters, it may be better to visit with your mom over the phone. Stick with me here. You know how it is, when your brother calls from Alabama and he has a perfectly wonderful conversation with mom. Then he shares with you how he thinks, "Mom is fine. She sounds great." Well, the reason they can have a perfectly wonderful conversation for 15 minutes is because Mom recognizes his tone of voice, but doesn't see his face. So she is talking to her boy.

The "boy" will not believe there is anything wrong until he experiences his mom face-to-face. So the next time you need to leave town suggest your brother stay with your mom for the week. Only when he experiences what you have been experiencing for months, will he believe there is something wrong.

A daughter was taking care of her mom. During the day, her mom would sometimes swear at her and not be very kind. But at night when her mom was in bed in a darkened room, the daughter would sit next to her and her mom would then turn to her and say, "Where have you been?" That is when she knew her mom recognized her. This daughter knew her mom despised chin hairs, and if she tried to take them off during the day she would get yelled at. So at night when her mom recognized her tone of voice in the darkened room she would say, "Mom, I see a couple of chin hairs." And her mom would respond with, "Get them off. Get them off." And Mom would thank her for getting them off. As the saying goes, all's well that ends well.

So, daughters and sons, when you come in to visit your mom bring a picture of yourself when you were four years old. Be sure to kneel down when visiting, because then you become small, and they may have a moment of recollection because they see you as a child. Call your mom by her first name instead of saying, "Mom, do you remember me?" As soon as you say "mom" they may become confused. "Alice, I found this picture of Ginny in the attic. She was quite a tomboy. She liked to climb trees in that pink dress you made her." Ginny can give her mom her memory back without her mom saying a word. And you never know, Ginny might hear stories about herself she never heard before or quite possibly her mother might say, "I love her."

They may not recognize you but they have not forgotten you!
– Jolene

Newfound Feelings

Powerful Tools That Create Positive Outcomes

Love and care with a genuine heart
—Jolene Brackey

Remember Their Greatness

W hat is each person's greatness? What has brought the people you care for great joy throughout their lives? This is the key component to any person you are caring for, whether they have dementia or not.

Let me share with you one of my great joys. Softball. I have been playing softball since I was four and have four brothers who have made me a pretty tough softball player.

To create a moment of joy when I get dementia all you have to say is, "You're an awesome softball player." I'll smile. "I've seen you hit a home run." Yes, I have. Then to really create a moment, point to any man close to me and say, "See that guy over there. I bet you could kick his butt any day of the week." Yes, I could!!!! And you need to say "Kick his butt," because those are the words I use when talking about softball.

Now you're thinking that you could buy me a softball glove to hold during the day. I might compliment you on the glove...but I won't want to keep it. The glove I want and need is mine. I have had my glove since ninth grade. And you know what…it stinks, literally! Yea and it will probably stink up my room like it stinks up my car. But it's not about you…. it's my room and it's about what brings ME comfort. My glove will forever bring me true comfort. You can't put a price on that.

My glove is the same as another's favorite chair. Maybe it has a hole in it, and it doesn't look or smell the best. But it's not about you . . . it's about what brings this person true comfort. Her favorite chair NEEDS to be moved with her no matter what it looks like. We all have a favorite chair. What if someone told you when you moved that you couldn't take your chair. How would you respond? People with dementia are responding through their actions, but we just haven't figured out what comfort items are missing.

My glove is also the same as someone else's favorite outfit. Yes, her favorite outfit has a few holes and may smell, but it is the outfit that brings her comfort.

After presenting a seminar, a lady approached me and said, "Because of you I am going to let my mom wear her nightgown everyday with no underwear underneath it." I said, "YES!!!!!!!!" She continued to explain how she had been fighting this battle with her mother for almost 10 years. Her mom persisted to wear her old nightgown with everything. She simply decided that day she didn't want to fight with her mom anymore.

The other pastime that brings me great joy is playing cards. I could play cards 24 hours a day, 7 days a week if someone would just let me. I love the game 500. When I get dementia I may not be able to play a perfect game. But if you corrected my game, would that create a moment of joy? NO!!! If you beat me, would that create a moment of joy for me? NO!!!

We need to let go of our expectations of how they should play, and let them feel like they won every time.

During a seminar, this gentleman pointed out that his wife was just like me. She loved to play cards. But when he asked her, "Would you like to play cards?" she didn't respond. He would ask a few more times with no reaction from her. Then he would take his cards out of his pocket and show them to her asking, "Would you like to play cards?" She would take the cards, go over to a table, deal them out. I interrupted, "You let her win didn't you?" He replied, "She plays a perfect game, as she always has, and beats me every time."

Frequently they stop doing "their greatness" in the beginning stages of Alzheimer's, because it causes them frustration. A good time to give back their greatness is when they are in the middle stages. This is the time when they don't think anything is wrong with them. In other words, they don't remember that they don't remember.

What we put back in their hands may possibly trigger their whole memory on how to do something!

They may not understand the words that come out of your mouth, but they might understand what you put in their hands. We need to give them their stuff back!
—Jolene

powerful tools that create positive outcomes

Newfound Greatness

Live Their Truth

No matter how hard we try, we cannot bring back her short-term memory. We can, however, take hold of her long-term memory and use it to create moments of joy.

This means we need to live her reality. When she is looking for her mom, we need to give her an answer that assures her that her mom is perfectly OK. You could say, "Your mom is in the barn feeding the chickens. Your mom is in the garden." By giving answers that make sense to her, she is able to relax and not worry about where her mom is.

Under normal circumstances, it seems like you are lying. But these are not normal circumstances. This is a disease. I reassure you it is not lying, but it is "living their truth." I would like to ask you a few questions. Would you ask someone right now where your mom is if you knew she was no longer living? Would you ask someone where your horse is if you knew you didn't have a horse anymore?

A person wouldn't ask these questions unless it is very real in her mind. This is her truth and we need to live in her truth. Guess who has to be the one to change. You do! They are doing the best they can with the abilities they have left. So do all you can to make whatever or whoever they are looking for seem perfectly OK.

Here is another way to look at it. You have Alzheimer's, but do not remember you do. And you think you are perfectly fine. You are actually 85, but think you are 24. You wake up every morning in a strange place. You remember you have children but you cannot find them. You ask a stranger who acts as if they know who you are, "Where are my children?" They tell you the truth: "Your children live in Alabama. You live here now. Everything will be fine." Your reaction would be: "Everything will not be fine because this is not my home, and I think you are lying to me. I want to go home! I need to find my children." What a panic you would create for that 24-year-old mother of young children.

The bottom line is this—*there is no reasoning with a person who has Alzheimer's,* and you will not be able to make them live your reality. Choose to accept, and everyone wins.

Jake would wake up at 4:00 almost every morning and insist he had to go to work. He was a construction worker most of his life and until people "lived his truth," he would become angry because all of these women were telling a man, "You don't have to work anymore." The better solution was to give him a reason why he didn't have to go to work at that moment. "It's raining out. Your crew called and said it's too wet. I will make you some coffee." Notice we didn't make him go back to bed, because his "habit of a lifetime" was getting up at 4:00.

Margaret would wake up in the morning and want to water her horse. I would whisper (because it's our little secret), "I got up early and did it for you. You can sleep in this morning." Now we all know what happens to kids when they don't do their chores. If I would have replied, "You don't have a horse anymore. You are 82 years old and live here now." In her mind she is thinking... "WHAT!!!! I lost my horse. My dad is going to tan my hide." Again, reassure her that her horse is OK. So a better answer might be, "Your horse is in the barn."

When a person says, "I gotta water the horse," you also need to think that he might need to use the bathroom. In their generation that was one way they used to say, "I need to go to the bathroom." Yes, it can get kind of confusing at any moment.

Do you know this is the only disease where you can make mistakes all day long, because five minutes later they don't remember it. That is a blessing! When they come around the corner in the next 30 seconds and ask you the exact same question, you get to keep changing your answer until you find the one that works.

People ask me, "How do I know if I have found the right answer?" Just look at the person's face. It will tell you everything. And if it works, it works. Don't question it, no matter how bizarre the answer seems to you. Your goal is to create a better reaction. You are not shooting for a perfect reaction but just a better reaction. When you find the answer that works to the question they ask 50 times a day...tell everyone!!! It is a treasure that will surely create a better day.

Imagination lit every lamp in this country,
built every church, performed
every act of kindness and progress,
created more and better things for people.
It is the priceless ingredient for a better day.
—Henry J. Taylor

Newfound Truth

Universal

Reasons

W hatever age our loved ones are living, we need to give them a reason why they don't have to do what they think they have to do. Give them a universal reason why or at least something that they may believe. Every person is different, so some of these answers will work and some won't. When you find the answer that works, write it down so everyone can use it. (Oh yeah, be sure to remember where you wrote it down.) ☺

Here are some universal reasons that might work:

Where are my children?
First you need to figure out what age she thinks her children are, and then how you can make them seem perfectly OK.

> *Your baby is sleeping.*
> *Your kids are in school.*

Sue is taking a nap.
Tom is working.

If their question 50 times a day is "Where are my children?" find an answer! The next time the children come in to visit, ask them where would they be after school, and what the name is of their best friends from school. Now we have a believable answer. The only person who can give us that answer is the child. It is worth our time to find the answer to the question they ask 50 times a day.

I have to go to work.

Find out what their occupation was and then give them a reason they would understand why they don't have to work today.

It's Saturday. (Not knowing what day it is becomes a blessing, because it can be Saturday every single day of the week.) P.S. "It's Saturday," won't work for a farmer. ☺

It's a holiday.

The boss called and said he wouldn't be in, so you are to take the day off.

The bridge/road is out. (Even if they fix the bridge/ road going into town, the bridge/road is forever out.)

There is a bad storm coming.

I need to go to school.

It's supposed to snow today so they cancelled school.
It's summer vacation.
It's a holiday.
OK, let's get dressed. (This answer is a good reason to get ready in the morning and then after breakfast, if they still want to go to school, you can use the answers above.)

Where is my mom?

Working in the garden.
Making dinner.
Doing chores.
At church.
Visiting_____.

You would think, "She's getting groceries," would work. But in their generation, mothers didn't leave the homestead very often. You need to figure out where she thinks her mother would be right now.

We tried all of the answers above but they didn't work for this lady. Finally we asked her son where his mom's mom would be during the day. He explained that his mom grew up in a boarding school and her mom would visit on the weekend. We found a treasure.... "Your mom is coming to see you this weekend."

Where is my husband?

Joe is at work.
Joe is uptown with _____.
Joe is out in the field.
Joe is at the hardware store.

Where is my wife?
> *Alice is at church.*
> *Alice is getting her hair done.*
> *Alice is visiting _____.*
> *Alice is getting groceries.*
> *Alice is making dinner.*

Avoid using pronouns such as he, she, they or it. The person with dementia usually doesn't know who you are talking about when you say he, she, they or it. Be sure to have the person's first name. Saying a person's name triggers a response.

> *My husband has Alzheimer's. We routinely used to do dishes together after every meal. When I say, "I need your help with the dishes" my husband doesn't get up. But when I say, "Sharon needs your help with the dishes," my husband will get up and help me. Saying my name triggers a response.*
>
> —Sharon

Another very difficult situation is when the person asks where his spouse is, and his spouse is deceased. Again, we need to live his reality. He would not be looking for his wife unless he thought she was alive. If you told him his wife is no longer living, it would be like someone telling you the same sad news. You would deny it. You would be angry because no one told you. You would have grief and depression.

Now imagine that you asked that question many times each day and kept receiving that sad news. It would impact your health, and decrease your functioning ability. I cannot stress enough that you should not tell the person that her spouse has passed away. Instead, think of what their spouse might be doing if they were alive. "Jo is at work. Jo is out in the field plowing. Alice is getting her hair done." Anytime you can fill in the names of people and what they would actually be doing during the day, your story is more believable.

While visiting a community a lady asked me in distress, "Have you seen my sister?" I responded with a usual response. "Yes I have. She said seeing she's looking forward to visiting you." She replied, "Oh thank God…because that lady over there said she was dead. I need to sit down. I am not feeling so well." People will have pain because of the answers we give them.

When you find the answer that works, write it down and tell everyone! Because if you don't, this is essentially what happens: She asks, "Where are my kids?" A caregiver replies, "They are at school."

She walks 10 feet and asks the next person, "Where are my kids?" That caregiver replies, "Well, I think Bob is living in Alabama and Shirley said she was going to take you out to lunch on Tuesday." "Tuesday!!!!!!!! I am not staying here till Tuesday. You get my kids on the phone!!!!!"

The person doesn't even remember the first answer and now is upset about the second answer. You need to write down the answer that works and tell everyone. You could write the answer down in a care plan, but realistically you can't leave the person to go find the answer.

A better solution is to have the answers written down in the room. Take a picture off the calendar of a subject they would like, e.g., an airplane, a kitty, a big red barn, etc, and hang it behind their door. Under this picture put a bunch of blank sheets of paper. When anyone—a family member, a caregiver, a visitor—finds the answer to that question they ask

50 times a day, they write it down. If they triggered a memory, they write it down. If they found a joke the person liked, they write it down. Anything that causes a positive reaction—WRITE IT DOWN!!!!

Here is one last little piece of advice. When you find the answer that works, make it as short and simple as possible. They not only lose the ability to talk in complete sentences, but they have difficulty understanding you if your answer goes into two or more sentences.

A farmer would wake up in the morning wanting to milk his 25 cows and the staff would assure him they had already taken care of the cows. It helped a little, but by the end of the day, he had 500 cows to milk. (My guess is the farmer thought they understood urgency in higher numbers). So one caregiver finally said to the farmer, "I was fed up with milking the cows so I sold them." The farmer replied, "Did you get a good price?" She said, "Yes." The farmer asked, "How much?" This was a tight spot now because she didn't know what they got for dairy cows back then. So she called her husband to find out more about prices and thankfully the farmer was content with her answer. She thought she had solved the problem, but the next morning he awoke with 30 chickens to feed.

If you can find a path with no obstacles, it probably doesn't lead anywhere.
—Frank A. Clark

Newfound Universal Reason

"I want to go home."

What if you were in a restaurant or at someone's house who you didn't know and said, "I want to go home." And they replied, "No, you live here now. This is your home. I am going to do your hair and we are going to play bingo. This is your home."

Wouldn't that make you feel scared, angry, and frustrated? You would want to dart out the back door as soon as these people turn their backs.

Well, that is exactly how a person with dementia feels. Now let's change the response to, "Oh, please stay for some dessert." We can all stay somewhere just a little bit longer (especially for dessert).

When the person says, "I want to go home," give them a reason to stay just a little bit longer and give them the hope that they can still go home. They can live in a place for two years and think it has been one day. That is why this answer works. A typical day might look like this:

When they wake up in the morning and say, "I want to go home."

Your response: "Let's get dressed first."

"I want to go home."

"But we are having bacon and eggs for breakfast. Just stay for breakfast."

"I want to go home."

"Let me do your hair before you go."

"I want to go home."

"We are going to have devotions soon."

"I want to go home."

"I just put on a pot of coffee."

"I want to go home."

"The church ladies have made us roast beef and mashed potatoes." (Triggers three responses: The food is good, the food is free, and it would be rude if they left.)

"I want to go home."

"But we are going to sing this afternoon. I love your alto voice."

Now men are much more difficult to get to stay. So when a man wants to leave, you need to become the damsel in distress. "Would you mind moving this really big box?" When the man gets up, take his arm and don't be surprised while you are walking down the hall if he thinks, "Dang…Where did I find this woman?" Walking with you down the hall is a moment of joy.

When you get to the box and he picks it up, the key words to say are, "You are sooooo strong." To get a man to want to stay, it may only take three statements. "You are soooo smart." And the last one. "You are sooooo handsome." Don't forget to wink. Men need to be needed in order to want to stay.

Another suggestion is to figure out what he would be good at fixing. What was his occupation? Then he needs to "help you" later that day.

This lady from New Jersey told me how her husband loved to fix the vacuum but every time he fixed it, she had to spend $120 to get it fixed. So she would hide it in the closet or in the basement. That just made him more upset because he couldn't find the vacuum. I suggested getting three vacuums from Goodwill; put one in every room and let him fix till his heart is content. You can't take away an obsession. You need to saturate obsessions.

At 3:30 it is really time to go home for the ladies because their kids will be getting off the bus soon, or they need to make supper. Figure out who they are worried about. If they are worried about their husband, "Bob, just called and said he has to work late." Or "Bob is having a beer with John." The next time her husband visits, ask him what he would be doing after work if he wasn't home. If she is looking for the kids, "Sally is playing at Ruby's house." When Sally comes to visit, ask her where she would be after school if she wasn't home and get the name of person she would be playing with. The more information you have the more believable your answer is.

Now at night when they look around the room and they don't recognize the place they are living in, they are usually thinking, "I don't know where I am at. If I don't know where I am at, my mom won't know where I am at." So we need to figure out who they are worried about and a possible response might be, "Your mom just called and she said it is too dark to walk home." Or "When your mom gets here I will come get you." Or "Bob just called. He has to work a second shift. He will pick you up in the morning."

At night when they are worried that their mom and dad won't find them, reassure them with this reply: "Get your rest. When your mom gets here I will come get you." Or "I called your mom and she is picking you up in the morning. We have a beautiful room ready for you."

What if at night you wondered where your parents were and someone said, "Your mom is no longer living. Get your rest dear." Could you get your rest? Obviously a better response would be . . . "Your mom called and said it was OK for you to stay the night." Your answer, no matter how bizarre it seems to you, needs to bring reassurance that everything is OK for the moment. That is the key!

> *My husband, Bob, would tell me he had to go home. I would literally have to get him in the car, take him up the road, come back by the house, and have him tell me where the house was. Then he was fine for the rest of the night.*
>
> –Shirley Larsen

When they wake up in the middle of the night frightened, a 77-year-old caregiver I met had the best answer. "Get your rest dear. I promise it will be better in the morning." The key word is promise. I also thought to myself, "That is what my mom would say if I woke up with a bad dream." It's not so much the words that come out of your mouth, but it's your tone of voice that leaves a secure feeling.

You also need to realize again they only know what they see right now. They wake up in the middle of the night and see this lady with grey hair and an apron. Who is she? Grandma. Who do with feel safe with? Grandma.

Now I would like you to imagine a man working night shift. Nice guy. When he walks into the room, what is she thinking? Intruder!!! If a man wants to work night shift he needs to wear a grey wig with an apron☺. Seriously, they only know what they see right now and what they see might be causing fear or comfort. Grandmas give us comfort.

Another response to, "I want to go home," is to start singing . . . "Show me the way to go home. I'm tired and I want to go to bed . . . " Then, give a little chuckle and say, "I like to sing that song, it makes me feel better." You should all know that song. It will lighten any situation.

The guilt families feel when they hear "I want to go home," sometimes compels them to move a loved one into their home thinking it will help. Know that even if you took them to your home, they would still want to go "home." The home they are looking for no longer exists. The best thing you can do is help them feel safe and secure in the place they need to live.

> *I dressed up as an angel one year for Halloween and walked into this person's room. The lady said, "Are you here to take me home?" I didn't know what to do so I left the room and told the administrator. The administrator encouraged me to go back in the room and sit with her. So I did and I simply said, "I am here. It is ok. I am here." The lady died within five minutes.*
> —Caregiver who gave an amazing gift

When they say, I want to go home, they might be asking for permission to leave this world. It should be OK to go home, but so many people hang on because no one has given them permission. Now if the person with dementia thinks they are 15 years of age or younger, they are not going to believe it is time to go. It is more difficult for a person with dementia to "go home." Hospice would agree.

After a presentation, a lady approached me and shared with me this story.

> *My mom passed away last Thursday. I wish I would have heard you 10 years ago. For the past month my mom has been saying in broken language that she sees her mom and wants her mom to come inside. I thought I was doing the right thing by replying, "Your mom will be in in a little bit." Last Thursday I finally understood and I said to my mom, "Go outside and play with your mom." My mom died within 2 hours.*

When the person is seeing other people who have already passed on, that may be another way of saying it is time to "go home".

—Jolene

Newfound Response to "I want to go Home."

Sense
of Belonging

Any human being would feel some level of fear and insecurity if they were in an unfamiliar place. Realize for some, the place they need to live will never really be home. So, maybe focus on making the situation seem temporary. It might be OK to stay a little longer until someone can take them home. If they feel this arrangement is temporary, they are more likely to relax and enjoy their day.

Sarah would ask 50 times a day, "Where are my children?" Now we knew Sarah had a strong work ethic, so the answer that usually worked was, "Ted is working downtown, and Shirley will pick you up at 5:00 p.m." Ted actually did work downtown, and if Sarah had a good morning she would be OK with Shirley picking her up at 5:00. If she wasn't having a good day, she would usually respond, "I raised and took care of those kids; they better take care of me. I am not staying here until 5:00." Because of her short-term memory loss she would come around the corner within 30 seconds and ask the same question to the same person. If she was upset, we knew we needed to change our response. "Ted is at work, and Shirley just called and said she is picking you up at 10:00 this morning." Then at 10:00 we would say Shirley is picking you up at 12:00; at 12:00 she is picking you up at 4:00; at 4:00 she is picking you up after supper; after supper she is picking you up at 8:00; at 8:00 she is picking you up in the morning. By now, you probably realize Shirley isn't going to pick her up. Shirley isn't picking her up until Tuesday to take her out for lunch, but that answer, to say the least, upset Sarah. Sarah was OK with staying a little longer, but she wasn't going to stay here until Tuesday!

This technique *should not* be used for someone who still has short-term memory. If the person is waiting by the door all day long, you know you made a mistake. Different dementias affect people in a variety of ways.

It seems to me that our basic needs, for food and security and love, are so entwined that we cannot think of one without the other.

—M.F.K.Fisher

Newfound Sense of Belonging

Stop Correcting Them

First let me give you Alzheimer's so you know what it feels like. Whhhooooooooshhhhh! You have Alzheimer's and you walk into a memory care community. You have no idea where you are (but you live there). You are walking around trying to find something familiar. You come across a purse that looks like yours. You pick it up so happy to have it back and then someone comes along and says, "That's not your purse, Alice." They take it from you.

So you walk on and walk into a room. Laying there on the chair is your sweater. You put it on and it feels good to be warm. As you walk out of the room, someone comes up to you and says, "Alice, that is Edith's sweater." So they take your sweater off. You are a bit tired and you see this nice comfy chair in another room. So you walk over and sit down. Immediately the lady in the room says, "Get out of my room! Get out of my room!" Now, you just want to go home, and you walk around trying to find someone who will take you home but everyone seems so busy. If you could just find your mom, she would make everything OK as she always did. So you head toward the door because you want to go home. You push on the door and an alarm goes off.

Would you want to stay in this place where people constantly corrected you all day long? "No, that's not your room." "No, those aren't your clothes." "No, don't go in there." "No, come back this way." Would you want to stay in a place where people corrected you constantly? "No!!!"

We need to STOP CORRECTING THEM. Would they be taking someone's stuff just to make you mad? No. Would they be wearing someone else's clothes because they want to wear someone else's clothes? No. Would they be in someone else's room if they knew it wasn't their room? No. This tells us they are doing the best they can with the abilities they have left. No matter how many times we correct them, can they change? No. Again, guess who has to be the one to change. Yes, it's still you. They really are doing the best they can with the abilities they have left. Their brains are dying. This is a disease. You need to change the way you respond because they cannot change.

When the person is in someone else's room, please do not correct, but simply say these magic words . . . coffee, coffee, coffee, cookies, cookies, cookies. "Hey let's go get some cookies". Or "Alice, where have you been? I have been looking all over for you." This makes the person feel needed. What is a reason they would WANT to come out of the room?

When you see them carrying someone else's stuff around, let the light bulb go on inside your mind, "She thinks that is her's. The next time relatives come in I am going to show them that doll and tell them to get

10 dolls for her." Why do we need 10? Because she will hide them, someone else will want to hold the doll too, and it might get damaged. Having backup saves so much valuable time. Now staff isn't looking for something that may take two hours to find. Time needs to be spent with the people, not trying to find things.

Guess what! You don't have to buy 10 purses anymore, because new technology has this thing you can attach to the purse and when it is lost just press the remote and it will beep. Follow the beep!

I believe there is a lot of unnecessary anxiety simply because the person with dementia doesn't see their purse or feel their wallet in their back pocket. We need to give them their purse back. Men have had things in their pockets for a lifetime. The top 6 are: wallet, keys, handkerchief, change, and a pocket knife.

Now I would like you to imagine he doesn't have any of these items anymore. How would that make him feel everytime he reaches into his pockets? Anxious. Insecure. Scared. Who suffers the repercussions when he feels all of these things. Everyone! Put back into his pockets what has always been there.

Pocket knife? He might stab someone. This person has probably had a pocket knife since the age of ten. He has been taught how to handle a pocket knife. This is a person with dementia, not schizophrenia. Who is the only teacher when deciding whether or not he can handle a pocket knife? He is! He may just teach you that the only time he uses his pocket knife is when he cleans his fingernails.

When you see her wearing someone's else's sweater, think, "Wait a minute, she thinks that sweater is hers." The next time family visits show them the sweater, and ask them to get 10 sweaters just like it.

There may be a lot of unnecessary anxiety simply because the person is cold. When I see a person wearing three sweaters and a coat, I think, "Yes!" At least they are warm.

Before you correct them, I want you to ask yourself three questions. Let's just take one of the toughest examples: wearing the same outfit every single day. 1st question...Does it hurt you physically in any way (not annoy you) that they wear the same outfit everyday? If you are answering honestly the answer is "No." 2nd question...Does it physically hurt any of the other people living here? "No." 3rd question... Does it hurt the person with dementia physically to wear the same outfit every single day? "No."

If your answer is no to those three questions, let them do what they want to do. Isn't that what you would want? It is difficult enough for them to get dressed once a day, let alone us trying to get them to change twice a day.

If the outfit is soiled. then, yes, now is the time to give them a reason to change clothes. Company is coming. It's Saturday night. Let's get cleaned up for church. Simply give them the reason they would get cleaned up for.

Take it another step and understand ... Understand if they are living during the Great Depression in their mind, they wore the same outfit every single day except on Sundays. Since they have short-term memory loss, do they remember they wore that outfit yesterday? No. And here is the most profound point I would like to make. Do they choose that outfit every single day because they like it? It makes them feel good. Allowing this choice defines "dignity." Don't you get to choose what outfit you want to wear? They should too . . . if it's not physically hurting anyone.

There was a dynamic-looking lady in a facility. She wore a striking pink dress, pink lipstick, pink rouge and pink fingernail polish with a white purse and white pumps. Her hair was every bit in place, and she walked with confidence. Because of her short-term memory loss and because this was her favorite dress, she always picked out the same dress. Staff and family had a real problem with someone wearing the same dress seven days a week. They also had a difficult time getting the dress off the lady to get it washed. Their solution was to pour coffee on it, so she would have to take it off. That was a horrible solution. This dress made the lady look good, feel good, and play good. She dressed to the hilt all by herself because this dress was familiar, and it triggered the experience of the glamorous process. Of course, the dress needed to be cleaned every once in awhile, but the answer isn't to damage it or tell the lady that she smells. Think how insulted you would be if someone told you that. If you think about her personality and body language, a better answer might be: "There is a handsome man visiting tonight. Let me wash your dress so you will look wonderful tonight."

When the person insists on wearing the same outfit every day, another possible thought might be.... show the outfit to the family and request they get 10 outfits that look a lot like the one they love to wear. So she will have 10 pink dresses in her closet. But please, please do not throw away the outfit they like to wear even if it does have a few holes and doesn't look too good. If you get rid of that outfit they won't (in their mind) have any clothes to wear. Too often families purchase a whole new wardrobe. I hear story after story of people who have done this, and the person only gets upset because now they don't have any clothes to wear and someone has spent their money. So sneak nine outfits in the closet and give one as a gift. The key words to say are, "I got it for 10 cents at a garage sale." In their generation if it didn't cost very much, they would wear it. If it cost a lot, they would save it for a special occasion.

But above all, before you correct them, ask yourself three questions. What they are doing right now—is it hurting me? Is it hurting anyone else? Is it hurting that person? If your answer is "no" to those three questions, let them do what they want to do. Isn't that what you would want?

You cannot control the disease. You can only control your reaction to it.

—Liz Ayres

Newfound Replacement for "No"

You Are Wrong, They Are Right

From this point on, you are always wrong and the person with dementia is always right. Think about it. If you are always wrong and they are always right there is nothing to fight about. If you are not fighting, there is less stress and if there is less stress, there is more success. Now, men, doctors, and preachers still get to be right, because in their generation men were right. Men....savor the moment, because when my generation gets there, it won't be the same.☺ There will be a whole new set of rules for the generations to come.

Does anyone have parents like this?

My dad will be telling a story about how on Wednesday they went to the sale barn. My mom will stop him and say, "No dear, it wasn't Wednesday. It was Tuesday." Then my dad will continue about how after that they went over to Harold and Stella's and had these really good cinnamon rolls. My mom will stop him and say, "No dear, it wasn't cinnamon rolls. It was this new kind of coffee cake." Do you think my dad at this point is going

to say to my mom, "Hey, thanks. You are so smart." No!
Essentially what is my dad feeling? Frustrated, angry,
and belittled. Is my dad's story hurting anyone? No.

I understand that story is pretty mild compared to some of the stories you will hear. But is their story is hurting anyone? Not usually. Please simply listen.

Listen to the emotion behind the story. Usually the facts of a story are off, but the way it shows how they feel right now is true. Respond to their emotion. If the emotion is anger respond with, "That shouldn't have happened! I'm sorry. I will discuss this with the boss." If their emotion is fear, "I am not going to let anyone hurt you." If the emotion is sadness, let them cry and a say, "I'm soooo sorry." Or say nothing at all.

Or, go ahead and fight with them. You can fight until you are blue in the face but who gets to lose in the end? You do. In fact, five minutes later, they have forgotten the fight and you are still steaming.

We need to take the word "NO." out of our vocabulary.

"No, Mom, you live here now, and Dad has passed away."
Replace it with: "Dad's at the hardware store again. He can fix about anything."

"I told you 10 times. Your kids aren't coming until Tuesday."
Replace it with: "Richard is at work right now." (Make them feel safe for the moment.)

"Helen, I am your husband. Don't you remember me?"
Replace it with: "Yea, your husband can be pretty stubborn, but he loves you."

"No, Dad, I am your son, John."
Replace it with: "Your son, John, loves to play the violin just like you."

"Shirley, your parents are no longer living."
Replace it with: "Your parents love you. They would not forget you."

"Mary, those aren't your clothes."
Replace it with: "Mary, company is coming. Let's get dressed up." Or, let her wear those clothes and return them to the rightful owner at the end of the day.

"Don't you remember?"
Replace it with: "You are right, I forgot."

"You already told me that story."
Replace it with: "I love your stories!"

"You are retired and don't have to work anymore."
Replace it with: "It's way too hot outside today to work. How about some lemonade?"

Excerpt from "Talking to Alzheimer's"

There are very few things that they can control, very few areas in which they feel any measure of independence. Where decision-making can be left to them, make sure they can keep it. Instead of seeing their resistance to something you want them to do as a personal affront to you, or as a foolish whim on their part, look at it as an opportunity for them to make decisions, to feel autonomous, to feel they are respected. What could be better for them?

When I took the word "no" out of my vocabulary, caring for my wife became easier because I wasn't fighting with her anymore.
           —A husband caring for his wife.

Newfound Right Made Wrong

"Give Me That"

Sometimes we really do need something our loved one, the person we're caring for, has. But we need to handle this gently and subtly. If you absolutely must take something away, replace it with something else.

> I have a little boy at home who is two years old. When he gets hold of a fork or another item I don't want him to have, I ask him to give it to me. Well, he doesn't. Then I try to take it out of his hands. Do you know this little guy is stronger than me? And he won't let go. So what do I do? I go get his favorite truck and start playing with it in front of him. He drops the fork, and now wants to play with the truck. I sneak the fork away and both of us are happy.

This principle also applies to people with dementia. Now this fork may seem like such a small thing to you, but all they understand and feel is a loss. If you absolutely must take something away, replace it with something else.

For example, that sweater someone is saying is hers. Before you take the sweater off the person with dementia, go get another sweater and say, "Alice, try this sweater on. It is much warmer." A bit of advice—don't ask them "Would you like to wear this sweater?" The answer is usually no.

When the person has an item that I needed, it worked much better to make them feel like the "hero" by saying, "Oh, thank you so much. You found it!" Then give them a hug out of thankfulness.

—Bonita Dehln

Again, ask yourself if what they have is hurting anyone. If your answer is, "No," then let them have it. If your answer is, "Yes," then replace whatever it is you are taking away with something else. Leaving the person with nothing leaves a feeling of emptiness and loss. Next chance you get, put something in their hands.

Do unto others as you would have them do unto you.

Newfound Replacement

The Rooster

I met a caregiver who said everyone thought she was nutty. You will find in the following stories, she was a little nutty, but it worked. If it works, who cares about being nutty? It might actually be fun.

There was a lady who did not want to get out of bed in the morning. This nutty caregiver knew this lady raised chickens, so she walked into her room and crowed like a rooster. Cock a doodle doooooo!!! The lady got up out of bed on her own.

A gentleman had a tendency to hit when staff cared for him. This nutty caregiver, who was quite small, came in the room, spoke like a child, and said with a hug, "Good morning, grandpa." She became the person he would not hit—a child.

You know the old saying "Think outside the box." With dementia this is a golden rule. Never assume something won't work. Too often, we play out in our mind the end result. But so often the end result is different than what we would experience. Experience truly is our best teacher.

Give them a reason THEY would understand to do what you want them to do. What are some trigger words, familiar sounds, or significant things that would help them to understand. It's not about what you understand, it's about finding "the rooster" that they would understand.

Experience is your best teacher.

—Jolene

Newfound Rooster Experience

Blame It On Something or Someone Else

Another wonderful way to make everyone happy is to blame everything on something or someone else—administrators, the environment, the doctor, the government, management. You don't want to take the blame for anything. You are the person who is caring for them so you want them to like you, to trust you, and to think you are on their side. They are more likely to cooperate with someone they like, so blame everything bad that happens on someone or something else.

- **Incontinence:**   It can be very embarrassing for them to wake up in the morning and find the bed is wet. Blame it on something else. "That roof is leaking again!! I can't believe it! I have to get it fixed." This answer really works! Now they think they didn't wet the bed, or they think they have you snowballed. If the person is incontinent during the day, blame it on something else. "You must have sat in some water. Let's change those pants so you'll feel better."

- **Taking car keys away:** If you have to take the car keys away, blame it on someone else. As a caregiver, you should not do it. Have a written note from the doctor. Or, if you are blessed to live in a small community and know the cops, use them. Ask the cops to take his keys away. Now when he gets home he is going to be mad....at the cops, not you. Of course, the next day or in 15 minutes he may not remember that the cops took his keys.

  So try something else....take the car to a friend's place and tell him that his car is in the shop. You may need to talk to the guy at the shop and make sure he backs up your story. If that doesn't work, try something else. Perhaps, one of the kids needed the car for the day. If that doesn't work, try something else. Replace real car keys with different car keys. If that doesn't work, try something else. If that doesn't work, try something else. Keep trying different solutions until you find the one that works.

  I would like to pass on some advice I have learned from other family members. Instead of selling the car, dismantle it so it doesn't run. Just seeing the car in the driveway can give them comfort. But if they no longer have their car, it can literally break their spirit.

  Note: A family member or anyone else can contact the D.O.T. and ask for the person with dementia to take a driver's test. The D.O.T takes his license away.

- **Forgetting appointments:** You know they have short-term memory loss, and to compensate you call 10 times in the morning to remind them of a doctor's appointment, and you also leave a written note on the refrigerator. When you arrive to pick them up, you begin by saying, "Are you ready to go to the doctor?" The answer usually is, "You didn't tell me. I am not ready to go anywhere."

Then, being only human, you tend to lose your patience altogether and say, "I told you 10 times and left you a message." Again this statement is an instant reaction expressing your frustration, but you are only making them upset, confused and reluctant to go with you. A much better response is to blame yourself for this misunderstanding. I told you it's hard to be wrong, but just do it. "Oh no, I forgot to tell you. I thought I did. I'm sorry. Let's go anyway and we can stop for ice cream, too."

Would you like another little hint? Don't take the time to remind them, but just apologize for "forgetting" and arrive early knowing they may need help getting ready.

If they catch you in a lie, or if they are angry, automatically use these words:

"I'm sorry."
"I didn't mean to upset you. It won't happen again."
"I forgot. I'm sorry."
"You're right. I goofed."
"I'm sorry. I misunderstood."
"I'm sorry I thought . . . ."

People generally won't stay upset with someone who seems genuinely sorry. It works. Don't try to reason with the individual, just automatically say, "I'm sorry." It's hard to fight with someone who is sorry.

> *Patient: Doc, I broke my finger in two places.*
> *Doctor: Well, stay out of those two places.*

powerful tools that create positive outcomes

Newfound Thing to Blame It On

Playing Favorites

What are their favorites? Favorite drink? Favorite temperature of room? Favorite snack? Favorite ice cream? Favorite sweater? Favorite place to sit? Favorite person? Favorite tease? Favorite blanket? Favorite place to visit? Favorite subject to talk about? Favorite music?

Avoid writing general statements like, "My mom loves to talk about her brother." Write down specific statements such as, "You have an older brother named Richard. Richard was smarter then the rest. Wasn't he? He walked you to school everyday." Simply write down her favorite things about Richard. Another detail might be, "When you visit, bring mom's favorite ice cream which is vanilla with butterscotch topping." Mail this list out to family and friends. It will help tremendously when they visit the person with dementia.

The following is an example of playing someone's favorites.

Emily Johnson

- Her favorite snack is buttered popcorn with lots of salt
- Her friends call her "Em"
- When she asks, "Where's my mom?", the best response is "doing the chores" or "she'll be right back"
- Favorite drink is chocolate milk
- Favorite painting is Starry Night by Van Gough
- Her favorite picture of her sister and brother when they were little is in the top drawer of the end table.
- "Em, you have gorgeous naturally curly hair."
- "Hey ornery" and lightly jab Em in the shoulder. (It creates a smile)
- Favorite songs Perry Como "Catch a Falling Star," "His Eye is on the Sparrow," "There is No Secret," and "Amazing Grace"
- Funny stories from Readers Digest make Em laugh
- Make sure the room is at least 69 degrees. If Emily is chilly get her green and purple afghan from the closet or her pink sweater. Em doesn't like a warm room. Cool with extra clothing is her preference.
- Favorite snack is softserve ice cream (but loves any kind of ice cream except sherbert)
- Sleeps in medium weight pajamas
- Loves a country drive

Be sure to find at least 20 things that cause a positive reaction such as; a smile on her face or a calm over her body. Then make copies of that list and give it to anyone and everyone who might be visiting or caring for the person you love.

A community told me of a lady who had to use the bathroom every 20 minutes and they made a list of 20 things that caused a positive reaction. Each staff person was required to do 5 things on the list during their shift. Guess what need went away? The need to use the bathroom every 20 minutes. When someone is screaming from their room, what are they seeking? Attention. When someone falls out of their wheelchair, what are they seeking? Attention. When someone is depressed in their room what are they seeking? Attention. When we do these things on the list what are we giving them? Attention.

When you are finding these treasures I encourage you not to play out in your head whether something will work or not. Your head is not your teacher, your co-workers are not your teacher, siblings are not your teacher, the state is not your teacher. The only person who can teach you what works and doesn't work is the person. So try everything! The person's facial reaction and body language will tell you everything you need to know at that moment.

> *When you get older, joy comes from birds,*
> *flower beds, and young people.*
> —Bruce and Rhea Fletcher
>
> *Newfound Favorites*

powerful tools that create positive outcomes

Let's Talk Communication

*Take things lightly and
you will fly.*
—Jolene Brackey

Be Like a Duck

Go with me on this. Just imagine you are a duck gliding across a pond, with not a care in the world. The sun is shining. The leaves are falling. It's a beautiful day! But what are ducks always doing underneath the water where no one else can see. Paddling! Paddling! Paddling! (OK, pooping, too. ☺)

We need to be more like ducks. On the outside we have everything under control. It's going to be a beautiful day. Then a person with dementia comes up to you and asks, "Where's my mom?" You are paddling, paddling, paddling underneath where no one else can see and you calmly reply, "She's doing chores."

If you hesitate or if your tone of voice is uneasy, the person will not believe a word that comes out of your mouth. And it's not really the words you say but it is your body language and tone of voice that they understand. If they see on the outside you have everything under control, it's going to be a beautiful day, then they are more likely to feel at ease with you.

Besides, wouldn't it be lovely to hang out with a flock of ducks who look like they have everything under control and who don't have a care in the world!

Be like a duck . . . keep calm and unruffled on the surface but paddle like the devil underneath.

—Unknown

Newfound Duck Paddle

Let's Talk Communication

Ninety percent of what they understand is not the words that come out of your mouth, but they do understand your body language and tone of voice. **Ninety percent!** That's a big number. Your tone of voice should convey a matter-of-fact, friendly, helpful, calm and respectful attitude.

Positive Non-verbal Communication

- Be aware of your body language and send a positive message
- Try a calm, gentle, matter-of-fact approach
- Reduce background noise by talking to the person in a place that is free of distractions
- Position yourself directly in front of him, at his eye level, and make sure you have his attention before you start to speak.
- Touching a person on the shoulder or holding her hand may help her focus on what you are trying to communicate

- Show the person what you want him to do by demonstrating
- Praise non-verbally through hugs, a caring smile, or a pat on the back
- Walk away and try again later with a different approach

Positive Verbal Communication

- Speak slowly in a low-pitched voice
- Enunciate your words
- Begin your conversation socially
- Use short, familiar words and simple sentences
- Talk in a warm, easy-going, pleasant manner
- Ask simple questions that require a choice of a yes/ no answer
- Listen carefully
- Give positive instructions and avoid "don't . . . can't" or negative commands
- Avoid questions that require short-term memory e.g.: "Did your son come to see you today?"
- Communicate using the person's long-term memory: "I hear you have a wonderful son."
- Give simple instructions for one task at a time (The simple task of brushing teeth contains 11 steps.)
- Keep talking to the person with dementia, even if he cannot talk back

Even if you no longer understand what they are saying, still respond as though you do. It's like when a toddler is learning how to talk. If you respond as though you don't understand, they become frustrated and keep repeating themselves until you do understand. It's human nature to want to be understood.

The person with dementia may not understand your words, or be able to articulate their thoughts with words, but they do know how they feel right now. Respond to their emotion not their words.

What give her inner world cohesion is not thought, but emotion. Garble is about emotion.
—David Dodson Gray

When we drive by the nursing home my little guy, Keegan, says, "Let's go see the peoples." When any little person is visiting be sure to give them something to share like a new toy, a bowl of fruit, flowers, a song, etc. On this visit my little guy had a new pair of cowboy boots. I knew that would work.

When we walked in a new gentleman motioned my little guy to come over to him. Keegan showed him his boots. The gentleman said, "Wow! Whoa!" Then Keegan stood on one foot. The gentleman said, "Wow! Whoa!" Then Keegan spun around in a circle. The gentleman said, "Wow! Whoa!"

I whispered into Keegan's ear, "Ask him what his name is." Keegan asked. The gentleman couldn't tell us his name. He couldn't tell us his name, but he made my little guy feel special in a matter of minutes. Who does my little guy want to visit now? The gentleman who only says, "Wow! Whoa!"

This gentleman taught me more about communication than anyone else. It doesn't take a lot words to make someone feel good. It may only take two words, "Wow!" and "Whoa!"

When you don't understand what they are communicating

- Listen actively and carefully
- Focus on a word or phrase that makes sense
- Respond to the emotional tone of the statement, not the word
- Stay calm and be patient
- Ask family members about possible meanings for words, names, or phrases
- Respond as though you understand
- Try a hug and change the subject
- Simply say, "Wow! Whoa!"

Things not to do

- Don't argue with the person
- Don't order the person around
- Don't tell the person what he or she can't do
- Don't be condescending
- Don't talk about people in front of them

People with dementia can hear, think, and feel emotions! Do not talk over, through, or about them as if they are not there. Avoid whispering because it arouses suspicion. Yelling into a person's ear who cannot hear very well will only upset or frighten them.

Excerpt from "My Journey into Alzheimer's Disease"

"The problem was not his hearing but the fact that it took two or three times calling his name to break through the fog. Of course, by the time it registered with him, he responded with irritation because someone was "yelling" at him. Now I (his wife) take extra care to gain his attention without raising my voice. I may

have to repeat myself and then wait for it to register. If this doesn't work, I may need to touch him to gain his attention. Never begin speaking to Alzheimer's patients before you are absolutely sure you have their attention. If they catch the last few words of your sentence, they do not have the ability to fill in the part they did not hear as we often do when we are healthy and this creates great confusion and irritation."

The person with dementia is frightened of making a mistake, losing his/her train of thought, or not finding the correct word to express his feelings or meaning. Conversation may come out as a jumble of words. Sensitive caregivers can assist by supplying words, finishing sentences, and listening carefully for connections and clues, and, of course, helping the person to talk as comfortably as possible for as long as possible.
—Moyra Jones

Newfound Way to Communicate

let's talk communication

Creative
Communication

Many times when having a conversation we ask questions like, "What did you do for a living?" This kind of a question requires the person with dementia to answer in a complete sentence, but he is unable to. It is our responsibility to turn our questions around so all he has to say is yes or no. He can say yes or no far into the disease. In fact, the last word a person with dementia can say is no. So the question should be, "Were you a farmer?" If he doesn't say anything, look at his facial expression. "Were you a businessman?" Continue through the different occupations until his eyes smile and that will provide your answer. If there is little response, fall back on the words, "I bet you were a hard worker."

Anytime you are trying to learn something about a person with dementia, communication is much more successful if you turn your questions around so all he has to say is yes, no, or nothing at all.

Richard would walk up and down the halls repeating, "I'm hungry, I'm hungry, I'm hungry." I walked up to him and asked, "What do you like to eat?" He just replied, "I'm hungry, I'm hungry." Reminding myself of this tool, I said, "Do you like warm chocolate chip cookies from the oven?" He said "Yes." "Do you like chicken?" He said, "No." "Do you like roast with potatoes?" He said, "Ah, hah." "Do you like noodles?" He said, "Could live without it." "Do you like carrots?" He said, "Oh, yea." The list went on and on and by the end I knew exactly what he liked and didn't like. Amazingly, his answers became more detailed and clear as we continued our conversation. This tool works, use it! At supper that night he would not sit down and eat. Guess what was for supper...chicken and noodles. ☺

A family member gave the best advice. He said that when he affirms his dad's conversation, whether he understands it or not, his dad is more likely to go into a meaningful conversation the son understands. In other words, he didn't stop his dad to correct him or say he didn't understand. The son simply acted as if he understood every word and eventually his dad's communication became clearer as they continued to talk.

The person is also more likely to communicate if you talk about a subject she knows WELL. If you can sense that she is struggling to communicate or unable to, take the pressure off by talking in ways that don't require a response.

Easy Talking Points

"This weekend we went to . . ."

"The weather today is . . ."

"I talked with your sister the other day and she said..." (Remember not to bring up something from short-term memory, just create general conversation.)

"At church this week the pastor talked about . . ."

"I have a dog named ____ and he is . . ."

"Someday, you will have to meet my daughter. She is . . ."

"You are such a good mom because . . ."

"You know when I was a kid we used to . . ."

Be aware the person with dementia may not understand a word coming out of your mouth, so when visiting it might be better to put something in her hands. Bring the person a gift, or some food, or flowers. People going through this are more likely to understand what they see. If she proceeds to eat the flower, that just tells you their development level is that of a one-year-old child, so whatever you give her should be edible.

Continue talking to your loved one, even if she doesn't talk back. Just because she doesn't physically or verbally react, it doesn't mean she cannot feel or receive benefit from hearing your voice.

Even people with closed eyes who do not speak can sense the closeness of another person. There are people inside all of them who need you now more than ever. Let go of your expectations of how you want them to respond and savor the time you have together. A moment of joy may come when you least expect it.

I walked into a dementia care center with an administrator, and there was a person with dementia who was shuffling along muttering noises. The administrator said she was in her last stages, a typical Alzheimer's person, and no one was in there. I walked up to that lady and gave her the biggest hug I could give—and she started giggling. Yahooooo!!!!! I created a moment of joy. Giggles are far better than nothing at all. Assume there is no one in there, and that's all you will see. Change your attitude and you will find so much more!

When you affirm their conversation, whether you understand it or not, you are more likely to go into a meaningful conversation that you do understand.
—A son's advice

Newfound Conversation

Quality Connections

D oes this sound familiar? You are walking down the hall and say "Hi!" to the first person, "How are ya?" to the second, and "Good to see ya." (with a pat on the shoulder) to the third person. Despite your good intentions, you are actually creating confusion while trying to connect with everyone that quickly. The first person is still sleeping. He doesn't even know someone greeted him. The second person is really nice and she responds, "Does someone need me. Who was that?" The third person is thinking, "Why would someone just hit me?" People with dementia cannot focus their attention quickly, so you have actually caused confusion.

When you want to make a quality connection with someone, you need to stop, get down to her eye level, make eye contact, and compliment, compliment, compliment. Say: "Joe, I love that hat on you." or "Alice, someday you are going to have to teach me how to sew. You are such a good seamstress." Or say, "Alice, your hair looks beautiful. Did you just get it done?" Alice may really have messy hair and look a little dazed. The least you are doing is making her feel better. Compliment them on the attribute that they like about themselves or on their greatness:

"I heard you can fix about anything."
"You are such a good fisherman. Have you caught many walleye?"
"So, you have a green thumb. Do you like roses?"
"I heard you love to dance. What about the waltz?"
"I heard you make the best rhubarb pie. I'll bet your husband loves that!"
"You are quite the charmer."
"You have a great sense of humor."

When you say something like, "Your hair looks great today." or "You must have been good at your work." you leave the door wide open for more conversation without putting people on the spot. A simple "Thank you." is all they need to say. This is because you made a comment; you didn't ask a question.

> *Complimenting a lady I said, "Your cheeks are so rosy." Without missing a beat she replied in a whisper, "Rouge, dear." Of course, she created two big smiles.*

> *I walked up to a lady who I didn't know, picked up her hand, and said, "Wow, you have really large hands for a lady." She beamed and replied, "Cause I did a man's work."*

Stop asking, "How are you?" You will either get a list of all the things bothering them, which could take 15 minutes to resolve, or they will have to reflect on how they really feel. Neither of these scenarios makes them feel better. Moments of joy will instantly happen if you break this habit and . . . compliment, compliment, compliment. Remind them who they are and give them their memories back. It takes 30 seconds.

Close your eyes . . . and go back . . . waayyyyy back:

I'm talking about hide and seek at dusk.
Sitting on the porch.
Hot bread and butter.
Penny candy in a brown bag.
Hopscotch, kickball and Annie I over!
Cowboys and Indians.
When around the corner seemed far away.
And going downtown seemed like going somewhere.
Being tickled to death.
Playing slingshot and Red Rover.
Climbing trees.
Building forts.
Running till you're out of breath.
Laughing so hard it hurts.
Licking the beaters when your mom made a cake.
Being tired from playing.

Didn't it feel good . . . just to go back and say, "Yeah, I remember that!" That's a quality connection!

Newfound Quality Connection

let's talk communication

Magic Words

When you are really upset about something, isn't it wonderful to have a friend to call who knows just what to say to make you feel better? We feel better when people around us are supportive, caring and thoughtful. Our troubles seem to lessen when we have others to lean on. When a person with dementia is troubled, try to think of magic words to make them feel better if you were in their shoes.

Examples of Magic Words

I will be here all day if you need anything.
Don't worry. I'll take care of it.
You are pretty important around here.
If you need anything, just let me know.
I do silly things like that, too.
Between the two of us, we will be OK.
You are a pretty special person.

Wow, you are so smart!
Thank you, I couldn't have done it without you.
That's a good idea. I'll have to try that!
You always look out for me.

Simply listening can be magical.

Modern science is trying to produce a tranquilizer more
effective than a few kind words.

—Unknown

Newfound Magic Words

Repeat, Repeat, Repeat

You are driving down the road and the person with dementia looks out the window and says, "Look at those beautiful trees." Thirty seconds pass: "Look at those beautiful trees." Thirty seconds later: "Look at those beautiful trees." This can go on for the entire trip.

Short-term memory loss only allows the person to know what he sees right now. He will repeat the same question, the same story, and the same statement possibly every 30 seconds. Here are some suggestions:

- **Patience, patience, patience:** Patience is a virtue, but you are human and your patience doesn't last 24 hours a day. Know that you CAN be human and have a really rough day where you didn't have much patience. Guess what? You get to start over tomorrow like yesterday didn't even happen because of your loved one's short-term memory loss. Every day you get to do it differently until you get a better day.

- **Distract rather than react:** Simplify a task she enjoys doing, such as: sorting silverware, folding clothes, sorting socks, peeling potatoes, organizing a tackle box, peeling oranges, shelling peanuts, or eating ice cream. Keep trying different kinds of distractions until you find the one that works—then it's your turn to repeat.

- **Short, simple responses:** "That's interesting. You're right. OK. I don't know."

- **LISTEN:** Listening without judgment gives dignity. Affirm their conversation whether you agree or even understand what they are saying.

All of these will work now and then. But you are human and will lose your patience, especially if you aren't getting enough sleep. You need to take breaks OFTEN! When you need a break, give your loved one a universal reason for your departure: "I need to go to the bathroom." This is a legitimate reason. Use it even when you don't have to use the bathroom, but just need time alone. Take naps when your loved one does. Eat well. Ask for help. Take time to do the things that bring you joy.

Try not to respond with, "You already told me that 10 times." When that slips out of your mouth, the time for a walk, chocolate, or a chat with a friend has arrived. Whatever brings *you* comfort or puts a smile back on your face.

They only know what they see right now.
—Jolene

Newfound Way to Acquire Patience

"The Spin"

When a person is fixated on a subject that is causing much frustration, I call it "a spin." Believe me—you do not want to go into their spin. Change the subject, walk away, or sing a silly song. But find a way to get the person out of this spin.

If you see by the person's face that he is really angry about something and you can't understand his words, don't try to figure out his spin. Just reassure him with, "That should not have happened. I'll take care of it for you." "I'll check on it." "We'll look into it."

If the person is asking for the phone book at any point, I can tell you they don't feel you are taking care of it, so THEY will take care of it.

Another option is to leave the room and come back five minutes later with a bowl of ice cream or a plate of cookies to help him forget about whatever made him angry.

You might think it's important to get to the bottom of the person's spin, so you can help resolve a problem. But you won't resolve a spin problem; the spin only gets bigger and bigger and bigger. Distract, listen, or leave the room and return with a different response.

A man said that when his wife would ask, "Where is my husband?" he would say, "Here I am." But that only made her angry. "Where is my husband? Where is my husband? Where is my husband?" she repeated with frustration. The only way to calm her was for him to go outside for a few minutes and walk through the front door calling out her name as he used to do when he came home from work. In that context, she quickly recognized her husband's voice and it brought comfort, rather than anger.

If people never did silly things, nothing intelligent would ever get done.

—L. Wittgenstein

Newfound Spin Cycle

Take Action!

If you see frustration in their face or if they are expressing anger, take action as though you will take care of it for them. "I would be upset too. I will talk to management about fixing it." You might have to take physical action and leave the room. Go get a drink of water or whatever it takes to be gone for a few minutes.

Other answers might be . . . "I will talk to your son about that. I will call your husband. I will call the doctor and ask his opinion." Now you don't actually call the doctor or her son. You are simply making the person feel like you are taking care of it, so they can stop fretting over it. Your answer should include the name of a person they trust or a person of authority so they feel like you have taken them seriously.

Act like you have everything under control (even if it isn't). They shouldn't have to worry about a thing. Wouldn't you love to have that feeling someday? What goes around comes around. Start today.

> *Don was in charge of a manufacturing company*
> *most of his life. He made frequent comments about*
> *how no one was working hard "around here."*
> *Don came to me and said something needed to be*
> *done about these lazy workers. I said I would get*
> *right on it. I didn't move with that statement, and*
> *he became quite angry with me. His wife explained*
> *that he had always been in charge of many people.*
> *After this understanding we acted as if he were our*
> *boss and responded with, "I'll get that done, sir."*
> *and took action by walking out the nearest door.*
> *Because of his short term memory we could walk*
> *back in within seconds; he responded better when*
> *he saw us take action.*

If the person becomes angry when you are giving care and he fights or yells for you to leave, do it! Honor his requests. Stop the confrontation and leave. Return five minutes later with a different approach (two cookies in your hand) and see if you get a better reaction.

Getting Robbed

A person with dementia becomes very suspicious. That is understandable, because they can no longer find their keys, purse, glasses, or jewelry. If the person is living in a care center, he has every reason to justify being robbed because someone takes his dentures, glasses, and clothes. A person might walk in their room in the middle of the night. People with dementia lose abilities, and they also lose the skills they need to adapt to changes. This means, then, that if something is wrong, someone else must be the culprit. When a person still lives at home, his or her caregiver is the main target. "You stole my money. A man was here and took all of my jewelry." (That man was her son.) To a person with dementia, strange people seem to be coming and going all the time because they can't recognize anyone anymore. Simply say, "That should not happen here. I'm going to call the cops." Now, don't go call the cops, but they need to see you "take action."

> *Doris came into the room and stated, "I got robbed last night." Our answer is… "I will talk to management, and we will tighten security. That should not happen here." Of course, you do not actually go to management, but it's important to make them feel like you are here to help. It's amazing how quickly they will let go of their concern. If we would have said, "Oh, it will be all right," they would have looked for another person who would listen to them. Think of it this way… how angry would you be if you told someone you got robbed, and they acted like it was no big deal.*

Taking action is a sign of respect. Give them that respected feeling.

Hallucinations/Delusions

When they are having hallucinations, first consider the medications they are taking. Different combinations of medication may be causing the hallucinations.

Their hallucinations are very real and just saying, "Alice, there aren't any snakes in your bed," won't usually solve the problem. Again, take action!

Pearl was yelling, "There's a fire in the house! There's a fire in the house!." Our answer was, "I called 911 and got everyone out. Come with me, I'll take you to a safe place." Then we walked Pearl outside. Sometimes it worked, sometimes it didn't. Was she ever in a fire? Consider her history.

She's still bothered a little by imaginary people telling her not to do this or that. So, when she tells me about 'him,' I tell her that we'll throw him in the river. Then I say, "Of course, sweetie, the river's still frozen and he'll go bump, bump, bump on the ice. She asks me, "Is that so?" And I say, "Yep . . . bump, bump, bump." And she laughs that beautiful laugh and we laugh together.
–Alan Ross, husband caring for his wife

This is a wonderful example of taking this lightly, adding a dash of humor, and the end result . . . a moment of joy.

Oh...I had a little chicken
And she wouldn't lay an egg
So I poured hot water down the little chicken's leg
Oh...the little chicken bawked
And the little chicken squawked
The little chicken layed a hard boiled egg
Dum Diddie Dum Dum
Dumb Chick
—Esther Svee Song/Sung to "Do Your Ears Hang Low?"

Newfound Way to Take Action

Illusion of Choice

If we opened their closet door and asked, "What would you like to wear today?" They may not respond because there are too many clothes to choose from.

Instead, pull out two outfits and ask, "Which one would you would like to wear—the blue one or the red one?" They still may not be able to make the decision, so give them a reason to choose one of the outfits. "I like the blue dress. It brings out your beautiful blue eyes." This is called an "illusion of choice." Another wonderful way to give an illusion of choice is to say, "How about I choose today and you can choose tomorrow."

We also need to give people with dementia an illusion of control to help restore their dignity. When we are passing out snacks ask, "Would you like a cookie?" instead of putting a cookie in front of them without saying a word. "Would you like to sit by the window?", instead of "sit here." If you are changing something in their environment, ask their opinion. In other words, make it seem like it is their idea. No one likes to be bossed around or overlooked, no matter what their age.

When the staff told Ray it was time to eat, he would usually refuse. But if they left the plate of food on the table next to him and walked away, the food would be gone when they came back.

Frank didn't usually want to go to bed at night when someone told him it was time to do so. So they asked him, "I wonder where your room is? Frank, can you help me find it? Is it this door? No. Is it this door? Hey we found it." For some reason, once he was in his room, he was easy to get into bed. The hard part was getting him there.

What a treasure this illusion of choice became. They were able to use this tactic over and over so everyone involved has less stress and more success.

> *Fear says I have to and I can't.*
> *Desire says I want to and I can.*

Newfound Choice

Kick Starting

When a person has Alzheimer's, he usually loses the ability to start a motion and locate certain parts of the body. We need to "kick start" him. In other words, if a person is sitting down for a meal and not eating, one reason may be because he cannot start the motion. Place your hand over their hand and assist with two bites. They might start eating on their own. If you ask them to put on their sock, but they don't respond, touch their foot and cue them again to put on their sock. It doesn't matter what the task is—if they respond blankly, start the motion and touch that part of their body to get them started.

One of my favorite things to do was give everyone lotion and encourage hand massages. When I asked Edith if she would like some lotion she would nod her head and then just sit there with a dab of lotion on her hand. I put her hands together and helped her rub in the lotion. After a short time she started doing it on her own.

Another way to help the person understand what you want her to do is by demonstrating the motion: you sew one pant leg while she sews the other. You put lotion on one leg, while she puts lotion on the other. Another method is cueing, which means to explain one task at a time as short and simply as possible.

Your goal is to help the person stay independent as long as possible. If the person is struggling, just help her with the task and let her try again the next day. They have good and bad days just like us.

Avoid helping too much. If you try to do everything for them, they will become more dependent on you, making it more work in the long run. Instead, allow them more time to accomplish each task.

A care provider was trying to get a gentleman to take out his dentures. This had become a daily struggle. Finally, she pulled out her dentures to demonstrate what she wanted him to do. It worked! He took out his dentures.

A care provider was struggling to put a Depends on a person. So she showed the lady what she wanted by putting one on herself. It worked!! The lady not only cooperated, but her attitude changed about wearing a "Depends." (Or call it underwear). ☺

When Mr. Evans came into the Alzheimer's facility, he functioned at a pretty high level. He was still able to do accounting-like work in the afternoon. I took maternity leave for about four months. When I returned, he was in a wheelchair and had declined rapidly. I asked the staff what happened. She said she wasn't sure, but now whenever she asked him to brush his teeth he just opens his mouth. I realize I didn't witness the decline, but the fact that he just opened his mouth making no attempt to brush his own teeth told me staff was doing too much for him, making him dependent on others.

Attitude
God guides my hand and
shows me again and again
how to hold the brush.
Yet each day He lets me choose the colors with which
I paint the canvas of my mind.

—Teresa Burleson

Newfound Kick Start

let's talk communication

Your Mood Affects Their Mood

You better believe it—your mood does affect their mood! If you're rushed, they are rushed. If you're upset, they are upset. If you're happy, they are happy. Basically you decide what kind of day it's going to be. I am not saying it's easy. We all have bad days—that's life! Know that you can have bad days. You are human, not perfect. Short-term memory loss again is a blessing. Even if you have a bad day, know that tomorrow you get to start over fresh. The person with dementia doesn't remember what happened yesterday.

People always say I have so much energy and I do. When I started working as an activity director in a Alzheimer's facility, I took my energy with me. I would enter the building all bubbly and hyper, talking loud and fast as I always do. I felt like I was doing my job if I kept the people busy all day long. Well the first six months, to say the least, were difficult. The saying "people were bouncing off the walls" came true. Wherever I would *go, they followed me. They weren't able to sit down and relax with me around. Luckily, I couldn't keep up the pace, and one day I said to them, "I need to take a break. I'll be back in 20 minutes. Relax and enjoy the peace and quiet." I returned in 20 minutes, and most everyone was still sitting and it was quiet. Amazing! My mood calmed down. I realized I controlled the stimulation level. My mood **does** affect their mood.*

Another tool to help calm people down is to sing two slow songs at the end of each stimulating activity or if they seem anxious. Sing songs like, "Silvery Moon" and "I'm Forever Blowing Bubbles." When you carry relaxing tools, you will be able to perform magic.

If you are a caregiver at home, one way to get started on the right foot is to ask a family member or hire someone to get your spouse bathed and dressed each morning. You can have a quiet hour to yourself, and then the two of you can start your day together, refreshed and ready to go.

Even if you are having a bad day . . . maybe your co-worker or a family member is frustrating you. You can still do this . . .

Go into a room and say with a smile and a giggle. "She is driving me crazy. I don't know what I am going to do." Giggle, giggle. "I hope she is gone tomorrow."

Remember, 90 percent of what they understand is not your words. What they understand is your body language. As long as your body language and tone of voice are positive you pretty much can say what you need to say, and YOU may get a better day.

Joys are our wings!

Newfound Joys

White on White

The clothes you wear do affect their mood. It's true. If you are wearing a white uniform and standing in front of a white wall, they see a decapitated head and hands coming out to help them. Scary! If you wear black you may seem like a hole in the wall or they think you have just attended a funeral.

Wearing bright mid-range colors like purple, green, bright yellow, and deep pink with lots of patterns helps the person see all of you. They might pick the flowers off your shirt but that is better than being frightened of you.

Don't take my word for it. Try it! One day wear the color of the walls and the next day wear something bright and cheerful. Who knows? You might get an unexpected compliment.

What color is the toilet? White. What color are the bathroom walls? White. What color is the floor? Off white. They resist sitting down because they don't see a toilet. Do you know what I learned with my interior design degree? Colored paint doesn't cost more than white paint. So, by painting the wall behind the toilet they are able to see the toilet in three dimensions. What color is the shower seat? White. What color is the shower stall? White. Placing a mid-range colored towel on the shower seat would help them see it. But what color are the towels? White. Hmm, do you see a pattern here?

If you are doing an art project with them and the canvas is white against a white wall, they may not see the canvas. It may be as simple as painting a purple outline so they see where to draw.

If you are wearing red or have red fingernails, some individuals may not cooperate with you. In their generation, red was the devil's color. Some men may not want to be seen with you, while others think this is a great opportunity. Of course, not all people are affected by the color red but it's something to keep in mind.

If you are wearing scrubs and taking care of them, they are confused. Do people with dementia think they are sick? No. So what are they doing in a place where people are taking care of them? When caregivers wear regular street clothes and act more like a friend or visitor, the person with dementia is more likely to cooperate.

What isn't tried won't work.
—Claude McDonald

Newfound Color

Look Good,
Feel Good, Play Good

I sn't that look good, feel good statement true for whatever you are doing—sports, job interviewing, church, or dinner out, etc. The opposite is also true. When we don't look good, we usually stay in the comforts of our home so no one will see us.

This concept applies to all human beings. Imagine if someone put a purple shirt on you and pants, but you really prefer dresses. Maybe all your clothes are too tight or have rips in them. How would you feel about socializing with others now? Clothing is one way we express who we are and what our personality is.

Sarah loved to wear red and chose to wear red every day. On the days that her red outfits were in the laundry, she had a green outfit. When she wore green I swear she wasn't as congenial. But on the days she wore red she looked good and felt good so she received more compliments. "Sarah, I sure like red on you." She replied proudly, "I do, too. My mother never let me wear it because she said it was the devil color, but I like it." Knowing her past, she was not very close to her mother, and she was the tomboy of the family. Seldom did she talk about her mother except when she was rebelling. So this becomes a wonderful story; a story we all can relate to. She should wear red every day.

What we wear does affect our mood. Why is it when a person gets old it becomes OK not to look good? Every morning be patient and allow ample time for the person to get ready for the day (comb hair, shave, lotion hands, apply cologne, apply lipstick and put on clothes they feel good wearing). So what, if they eat breakfast in their pajamas or eat breakfast a little later. Don't we enjoy the mornings when we get to "putter" around? Make it a priority to take the time to help them look good, so they feel good and then they will play well (function higher).

Puttering is really a time to be alone, to dream and to get in touch with yourself...To putter is to discover.
—Alexandra Stoddard

Newfound Favorite Clothes, Shoes, Hairstyle

Power of Touch

This chapter was written by Teresa Stecker, R.N., who worked for 12 years as a hospice center nurse.

Touch is one of the basic needs of life. The craving for touch to communicate affection, comfort, and reassurance is present the day we enter the world. As a newborn, touch is the first of our senses to be used to develop our sense of the world around us. The stroke of a mother's touch calms a baby's cry. As we develop, we seek and welcome meaningful touch through kisses, hugs, playful touch, holding hands, and other positive touches. Touch, like our other senses, gives us clues about the reality around us, our world awareness. It tells us if it is a safe world and a place where we are loved and valued.

Touch that shows anger, anxiety, frustration, and impatience brings tension, agitation and anxiousness. Touch that shows affection, reassurance, comfort, and value, brings calmness and peace. Touch has the power to break through the feelings you want to transcend. As we age, other senses may change and fade away but touch remains.

Touch can reach through the fog, confusion, and fear of dementia. Reassuring touch grounds those who are spatially disoriented, brings people back to their bodies, and increases their awareness in present time and space. One touch can affirm that they are not alone and they are valued by the person who is beside them.

We need to stop and think about our touch and what that means to the person and to those around you who are watching. Your touch may give permission to others to enter an unknown world of dementia. As with the dementia person, touch can break through the fears of the families. Families may be unsure of what to do, but when they see you touch the person, you are validating that the person is still there. When you do this, families are more likely to move in and do the same thing. Sometimes, our touch of affection isn't so much for the person as it is for the loved one who is watching. It communicates the compassionate and caring part of humanity. Observing powerful touch can completely change the way one thinks about touch.

As Alzheimer's progresses, the critical piece is to find the touch that was meaningful and positive in the person's life. That may be a hug, a kiss, stroking of hair, holding hands, stroking the forearm, touching the forehead (like taking a temperature), or a handshake. It may be dancing or playing "Ring around the Rosie." This touch indicates that you know them because you are touching them in a way in which they are accustom and comfortable.

Some would say that touch is personal and not everyone likes to be touched. Too often, we make decisions based upon what we would like. But it's not about us—it is about what the person needs. In my years as a hospice nurse, I have yet to discover someone who refused all forms of touch, especially those alone or without loved ones. It simply comes down to discovering the right way to touch, the kind of touch that brings the most positive response.

In the final days of life, Grace slipped into a semi-coma. In her restlessness, her husband of 40 years stroked her cheek and her forearm. Whenever he left the room, he planted a small kiss on her cheek. The family, in unspoken agreement, decided that Grace would know she was not alone by communicating their presence through touch. So, her children and grandchildren took turns holding her hand. In her final days, she looked peaceful—no frown, no agitated movement of extremities, her muscles relaxed and breathing easy. She died peacefully with her son holding her hand. Through the simple and significant acts of touch, Grace felt loved until her last breath.

Our hands—the tools of touch—are powerful. We can hurt with them or we can help with them. Our touch through our hands communicates how we feel inside and our affections to the outside world. You show your intention with touch, how you feel about that person. When you watch someone touch another person you can see if they value that person through their manner of touching.

Our hands portray our inside state:
Our love for others
Our sacrifice for others
Our suffering for others
Our anger for another
Our beliefs about their value as human being
Our fears
Our ignorance

We seek it as children—the touch that shows us affection and security—and I believe we seek it and welcome it as we move to the end of life. We want to sense that the world around us values us. Even in the business of our work and life, we need to be mindful that we stop and bring calmness to our body so that our touch communicates time and attention to the person. Touch can and should communicate the following to the Alzheimer's person: You are honored. You are important. You are not alone. You are valued. And we know that you are still there even when you don't look like it or respond like it.

A friend of mine visited her childhood pastor, who has progressive Parkinson's disease. My friend shared how, as a child, she would draw the same picture over and over again for him and he would always hang one of the pictures in his office. They had a special bond. Now her childhood pastor is in a nursing home crumpled in a wheelchair, unable to even open his eyes. On her last visit, she just so happened to bring one of the pictures she had drawn for him. While describing every detail, she placed her hand between his hands. He didn't verbally respond or open his eyes, but a tear came down his cheek. His wife commented on how people don't visit him anymore, because he doesn't respond. This moment was a complete affirmation that he is still in there.

My first two weeks 18 residents met my gaze with an icy catatonic glare. I would smile and ask them if they wanted to participate in some new activity.

The answer was always the same. The answer was always "no." So I began giving massages. I found myself thinking, if I was in their situation what would I like? A massage would be nice. I brought in bottles of scented oils and lotions. I began rubbing their shoulders, necks and hands and as I massaged, I felt their armor fall away. At best, I am a stranger to them. I am not their daughter or a nurse. I am more like a familiar, nameless friend. Sometimes I am "Mrs. Yoo-hoo." Sometimes I am "Hey, Hey, Hey, You!" No one knows my name. But they know me. They know my spirit.

—Sally Dutra

When we were little and visited my grandpa, we would say, "How ya feeling, Grandpa?" He would reply with a smile, "With my fingers." As he grew older, he lost his ability to respond verbally. But one day, I said, "How ya feeling, Grandpa?" And to my amazement, he replied, "With my fingers."

—Granddaughter

Honor me with touch
Comfort me with touch
Value me with touch
Love me with touch

—Teresa Stecker

let's talk communication

Newfound Touch

Be Like the Sun

There was a sun and a cloud in the sky and they were fighting over who was the most powerful and the strongest. There was a little boy walking on the sidewalk and the cloud said that whoever gets that jacket off the little boy wins. So the cloud said, "I'm going first." The cloud floated over to the boy and started to blow. He blew and he blew, trying to blow the jacket off the little boy. What did the little boy do? He held on even tighter to his jacket. The cloud blew and he blew. Eventually, the cloud lost all his energy. He was tired and couldn't blow anymore. He turned to the sun and said, "All right, I give up. Give it your best shot." The sun didn't move. He just waited and warmed up. He radiated his warmth. He was very patient. The little boy started to sweat. The little boy thought, "It's getting warm out." So the little boy took off his jacket.

The moral of the story is whenever you try to force anyone in your life—your spouse, your kids, or the person who you are caring for—to do what you want, they hold on even tighter. But if you are more like the sun and radiate your warmth, have some patience, and, here's the kicker—give them a ***reason they would understand***, then they are more likely to cooperate with you. Not always, not every day. You are more likely to get a better reaction if you act more like the sun.

If you only remember two words two months from now, these are the two words I want you to remember: Be like the Duck and be like the Sun. Duck . . . Sun . . .Ducksun . . .Ducksun . . . Ducksun. And have some fun!

> *Be like the duck and be like the sun.*
> *It may just change your life.*

—Jolene

Newfound Warmth

Memory Enhanced Environments

Don't wait for the roses,
stop and smell the daisies
                    —*Jolene Brackey*

It's Time to Move

When a lot of us think about moving we just stiffen up and grow tense. It's no easy task when Mom or Grandpa must move—and it's not his or her idea. No one is going to say, "OK, I am ready to move." Usually, you are going to have to make the decision without their approval.

Any move is very difficult, whether you have dementia or not. You can expect it to take at least six months to adjust to a new place. Your family member is likely to be angry and insecure for a while. Take comfort in knowing this is a phase, and this too shall pass.

To ease the adjustment of moving, I strongly advise you to move everything prior to your family member's arrival. Take the person to a park or on a country drive while other people move their belongings. The goal is to reduce, as much as possible, the stress that comes from moving.

When moving, make sure you move three things.

1. Place of comfort
Where is their place of comfort? The sofa in the garage?

The kitchen table? The sewing desk? Whereever their place of comfort, be sure to take a picture of it, pick it up as closely as you possibly can and drop it into the place they are moving into. The kitchen table may be more important than her chair in the living room.

If the place of comfort is her chair, what side is the end table on? Right-hand side? The end table needs to stay on the right-hand side. When you rearrange their place of comfort the confusion will rise. When you buy them something new, it isn't theirs. If it isn't theirs, they aren't going to find comfort in it. The things that bring us comfort are the things we have been using for a lifetime.

> *A lady shared with me how she moved her dad into their three car garage and she remodeled the garage to look exactly like the first floor of his house. The paint on the wall was the same. The coat was still hanging behind the door. The bathroom was in the same location. The old recliner was there with the end table on the right hand side. She tried not to change anything and she said, "My dad didn't even know he moved." So where does his independence stay? The same.*

2. Their greatness

What is their greatness and where would they look for it? If you know they like to read and you put all their books on a book shelf, but they remember their book being under their pillow or on the end table, their body is not going to look on the bookshelf to find their book . . . their body remembers to look under the pillow. If you put their sewing supplies in a plastic container and put it in the closet, is she going to know where to find it? No. The sewing bag needs to be on the left-hand side of her chair because that is where it has always been.

3. Their bed and everything around it

What kind of pillows do they sleep with? How many blankets? Which blanket is their favorite? What has to be on the end table for them not to think they have to get up? Which side of the bed is the lamp on? Did they wear socks to bed? Are the covers tucked in? If you go buy a new comforter, whose bed is it? Not theirs! So then we have staff taking them into their room, they look around and decide this isn't their room so they leave. Staff brings them back in their room . . . they leave . . . bring them back . . . they leave. All of this could be happening simply because nothing in the room is familiar.

> *A daughter shared how her mom wouldn't sleep in the bed. She even bought a new purple comforter to put on the bed since her mom's old purple comforter wasn't looking too good. Not until she brought her mom's orange and green afghan and placed it at the end of the bed where is had always been, did her mom start sleeping there.*

If the person has lost her short-term memory, you may want to make it seem like staying here is temporary. For example, you might explain that the move is just for the winter, until the doctor says you are feeling better, or just for a little while. Your loved one's short-term memory loss can work as a positive in these circumstances. The person with dementia can live in a place for two years, but believe she has been there for just a few days.

Also, be aware that you probably are bearing the brunt of their frustrations. When you aren't there, she may actually be doing pretty well, but when you visit all you get are negative responses. If this is the case, ask staff members what they are observing. The answers may surprise you and/or even reassure you.

Another quick hint to ease the transition is to introduce the person to the other residents as if they were your friends (which eventually they will be). Help the person create relationships with other people by finding common areas of interest. Make an extra effort to share with staff, other residents, and frequent visitors their stories, their greatness, their hobbies, and their history. Knowing something about someone creates connections, which in turn creates new friendships.

Avoid making the statement, "You are here so they can take care of you." For the most part, people with Alzheimer's don't think they are sick. A better response would be: "She would love to hear about your doll collection." Or, "He knows a lot about farming, too."

When you get through the transition, share with other families your mistakes and successes. My hope is as you watch other families struggle, you will extend a helping hand with words of advice, affirmation, and assurance. Be the one to help people who have just moved "here" to feel welcome in their new home. Your attitude about this new home and the other people who live there is contagious. What message are you sending?

Here are some magic words a doctor and wife used together when it was time to move.

The doctor said, "I know you don't like the idea of moving to _____. But your wife and I are worried about you. We are not doing this to punish you. What is happening right now is not your fault. We love you and are trying to do what is best.

Affirm their feelings. Affirm that it is not their fault.
Affirm your love.

Newfound Mistakes and Successes While Moving

Pack Your Suitcase

Whoen considering how much and what clothing to bring, keep in mind the specific needs of your family member. For example, bring sweaters if your family member is usually cold and likes to wear sweaters. Elastic waists are helpful because the person can still wear the same clothes even if his weight fluctuates. These pants are also easier to put on and take off.

Provide a wardrobe that can be mixed or matched, but avoid bringing anything that requires dry cleaning. Choose the clothes the person likes to wear because clothing absolutely affects his mood. If he is reliving his days on a farm, he may feel more comfortable in overalls and boots. If she has always worn dresses, you probably won't include any pants.

We face new problems and new frustrations every day. But we either find solutions or ways to minimize and cope. This reminds me of early stages of Alzheimer's when she began to need help dressing. Panty hose were the biggest problem. I wish I had kept notes of all the things one can do wrong with putting on panty hose. Very soon that was no longer a problem. We did away with panty hose and changed to knee high socks. Brassieres were the next to go. There are lots of ways to simplify and "It's Not All Bad."

—Paul Edwards, husband and caregiver

The following is only a suggestion for the amounts of clothing to provide:

Women: Bring eight pairs of underwear, five bras or T's, five slacks, five blouses or dresses, one bathrobe, and eight pairs of socks. Socks should be same color and style that the person likes so it is easy to keep separated from other residents' socks. Additional items include three sweaters, two pair of slippers (the same kind and color), one heavy or lightweight coat (depending on the season), and two pairs of walking shoes. The shoes should also be the same in case one is lost. Also provide a pair of simple-soled, slip-on shoes that are comfortable and can be washed frequently.

Men: Bring eight pairs of underwear, five undershirts, five slacks, five shirts, two belts or suspenders, a bathrobe, and eight pairs of socks. Socks need to be the same color and style to keep separate from other residents' socks. Additional items might include three sweaters or vests, two pairs of slippers, one heavy or lightweight coat (depending on the season), and two pairs of walking shoes; avoid tennis shoes with side soles and laces because they may cause the person to trip. Instead, buy simple soled, slip-on walking shoes that are comfortable and can be washed frequently.

LABEL EVERYTHING!
Everything gets lost. Here today, gone tomorrow. There is no truer statement when it comes to Alzheimer's.

We had our share of things getting lost, but soon we learned that "Nothing is lost, it is just misplaced."
—Paul Edwards

Newfound Garments

Create a
Safe Haven

If someone came into your home and took all the items that are significant to you, would you want to live there? Would you still find pleasure and enjoyment being in your home? The things you choose to have in your home make it your safe haven because you are surrounded by things that bring you comfort.

Decorate with items that define who this person is, so when people enter his room, they see a unique human being and instantly know something valuable about this person. What are his hobbies or favorite pastimes? What subjects does he know a lot about? What items is this person familiar with? By filling his life with what makes him a unique individual, memories will flow when he enters the room because it is filled with things he knows and loves.

For instance, if a person's favorite pastime was fishing, find a large, detailed picture of his favorite fish and hang the lure that he would use next to the picture. Bring in his favorite fishing pole, fishing hat, and tackle box and place them in his room where he could easily see them. Avoid placing significant items in the closet or drawers, because if he can't see it, he won't remember where you put it. Better yet, think about where this person would look for the things that bring him joy and put it exactly in that spot.

A lady in one my conferences shared how she loved chocolate. OK, so that is pretty normal. But then she proceeded to tell me how she would put her chocolate in a small box. Then she would put the small box behind a large box on the top shelf of her closet, so no one else could find it. Now I am thinking, "What if she gets dementia and we find her standing on a chair in front of her closet reaching up to the top shelf?" Well, we are going to blame it on dementia, but really, she is going to the place where she has always found chocolate. What if she wrote this down and we knew to put chocolate in her closet on the top shelf. She goes to her closet to look for chocolate and discovers her favorite thing is still there! What a joy that would be!

Another example might be a person who loved to make quilts. Place a beautiful quilt on her bed or on the wall, and bring her sewing basket filled with spools of thread, fabric pieces, patterns, measuring tape, and so on. She can no longer make a quilt but she can still feel the fabrics in her hands, cut out shapes, look at a quilt that is not finished, and talk about her plans to work on the quilt next week. Remember to keep her significant items in the container where they have always been, and place the container where she would normally look for it.

Other items that are essential to create familiarity in the individual's room include her favorite chair (yes, even the ugly one), dresser, bed, favorite bedspread, significant possessions that trigger memories and other "stuff" that offers comfort. Again, avoid buying new furniture or decorations to make the room beautiful, because the individual will not recognize this as her room. Despite your best intentions, new furnishings will add stress while old, familiar items bring comfort and security to a new setting.

A lady talked about how she wished she could bring in her mom's favorite swivel rocking chair but the care center did not allow it because of the risk of falling. In my opinion, every effort should have been made so this mom could have her favorite chair to sit in during the day. Risk-taking is a normal part of life. Answer this question—what if you were moving and I said you couldn't take your chair with you? How would you feel about the place where you are moving? We need to fight for our loved ones. When you do, you are fighting for yourself because someday you might have to live in a care center, too.

Placement of decorative accessories matters, as well. The items on the wall should be hung about five feet above the floor or wherever her line of sight is. They should be able to see and touch their belongings. Seeing and touching their belongings bring comfort. The more comfortable they are, the more content they will be.

A lady moved into a facility, and she explained how she hadn't moved in yet. She actually was moved in except for her favorite chair and that was how she expressed that something significant in her life was missing.

A gentleman who used to be in the Army would wake up in the morning thinking he was in an army barracks because his room didn't have much more than two beds. Being in the Army didn't trigger fond memories, so this environment may have caused a level of fear. You could also get this person to stand straight up and march by saying, "Attention! March!"

And, as a side note, we all know moving to a smaller space presents challenges. What do you keep or pass along to family? Usually, lifetime accumulations lead to a surplus at the end—even after sorting through our loved one's possessions several times. Instead of selling the person's belongings at a garage sale, donate the "stuff" to a care center. I'll bet the belongings your mom has collected over the years would bring joy to many people.

Another hint when you're deciding what to bring to your loved one's new home is to recall her lifetime habits. For example, with bed supplies, does she like one or two pillows, feather pillows or regular pillows, several blankets or just a few? Or, is she more comfortable with a quilt or a plain comforter for her bedspread. Recalling her preferences will help you decide what items to bring. Remember, each person is different.

By filling their life with significant items, you are reminding them of who they are. These items you bring may get lost, damaged, or used by other people, 15 people have 15 rooms. They cannot remember which room is theirs, or what stuff is theirs because of short-term memory loss. That is the advantage of an Alzheimer's specific "home"—you could have three people in the same room doing three different things—but usually no one is bothered by any of the activities.

However, when a person with Alzheimer's lives in a place with other residents who are cognitively fine, it can be extremely difficult. A person with dementia is more likely to be rejected, corrected, or avoided. People with dementia actually function higher when they are with other people with dementia. In fact, you may observe a conversation between two people with dementia that no one understands, but they are truly enjoying one another's company.

Allowing people with dementia to have the freedom to wander and explore all corners of their home is a simple joy we can choose to give.

*We cannot give them their memory back,
but we can give them an experience that triggers memory.*
— Moyra Jones

Newfound Treasures That Bring Comfort

memory enhanced environments

"Where's My Room?"

It is very difficult for people to find their rooms, and rightfully so, because all the doors look alike. Have you ever noticed in retirement communities how people have distinct decorations outside their door? Most people are able to figure out ways to distinguish their doors. However, people with dementia usually do not have this ability. So it's even more relevant that we create as many clues as possible.

To distinguish his door from the others, hang items he is attracted to on or beside the door. If he flies airplanes, hang a picture of his favorite plane. If she likes a certain actor, hang his portrait. The person's name or signature should be about four feet up from the floor, so it is near eye level. Some people recognize their signature far into the disease. Hang up their favorite hat. Hang an 8" X 10" portrait of the person when they were younger to the side of their door .

Be sure to ask the person what he sees in the pictures before you hang them because she may see something completely different than you.

A lady I was visiting loved roses and outside her room was a picture of a lovely red rose. I complimented her on the picture and she said, "I don't like that. It's a mule's butt pointing right at me."

Below is an example of a door decoration of someone who enjoys fishing.

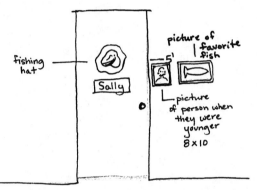

If you see someone wearing your Dad's fishing hat, smile because the hat is bringing moments of joy to two people.

Pat loved to fish in her younger years and that was something to be proud of in day. She had a picture of herself holding a 30 lb. salmon on a distinguished looking dock. This picture was hung right outside her room, and when anyone entered the facility, she would show them the picture and talk about how big the fish was. When Pat could no longer communicate very well, she would point at the picture, nod her head and her eyes showed you how proud she was of that day. Her room was also decorated very beautifully and the other ladies enjoyed being in her room, too.

Hanging significant items will enable anyone to remind them who they are.

—Jolene

Newfound Door Decoration

memory enhanced environments

Sparking Fond Memories

Our five senses are the closest connection to our memory. When you *smell* cinnamon rolls you think about the cinnamon rolls grandma made. When I *say*, "I'd lose my head if it wasn't attached." I think of my mother who said it often when she couldn't find something. When you *see* a certain flower you may think about a certain person. When you *hear* the train whistle you remember running beside the train waving at the conductor. When you *feel* a silky pink fabric you think about a favorite dress.

Realistically, we can no longer ask them to make a casserole, but they can wash off vegetables, taste different foods, talk about favorite meals and hear a prayer before they eat. When we surround them with things that trigger their five senses, we are ultimately triggering their long term memory.

Joan and Ray met at a singles group. Ray asked her what she thought of the group. Joan replied, "There's just a bunch of losers here." Not long after that, they started dating and eventually got married. So, faithfully, twice a year, Ray sent her a dozen roses with a note that said, "From the loser." Ray was diagnosed with Alzheimer's before the age of 52. Joan kept him at home for a long period of time. They would go grocery shopping together, and one day Ray wandered off. When she found him, he was in the flower department. She asked what he was doing and he stated, "Want buy." "You want to buy some roses?" she asked. He nodded. He wasn't able to figure out how to pay for the roses so Joan bought them. They took the roses home and put them in the vase. The next morning he walked into the kitchen and questioned the roses. She said, "You bought them for me last night, remember." She saw a light in his eye and he replied, "Oh yea, they are from the loser." She cried. Not moments later he was "gone" again. But she opened the window to his memory for a moment.

A facility would have tea parties. When the ladies saw the tea set and smelled the tea, they would sit up straighter, point out their pinkie finger, and socialize with one another. They were given an experience to trigger their memory on how to act at tea parties.

A gentleman who had Parkinson's disease went into a comatose state, and many different methods of therapy were being tried. The most effective therapy was to constantly remind him in conversation and through touch who he was. He was a basketball coach most of his life and loved the game. His therapy was to address him as "coach," talk basketball with him, and put his hands on a basketball. The family said this is the therapy that "brought him back."

If they are in bed most of the time, we can place things outside their window that they would enjoy looking at: a dog house (no need for the dog if you wish), bird feeders, small windmills, bird houses, fake animal figures, flower or vegetable garden, hanging plant, old bicycle, tractor, the American flag (Yes! Yes!) and the list goes on.

Another way to trigger memories is through our conversations. Conversations about outhouses, wood stoves, first radios, first kiss, holiday traditions, wedding day, raising children, the first dollar they earned, or memories of their parents. When we talk about subjects from their childhood, memories trickle out. When they can no longer verbally communicate, we can still give back their childhood memories. If you don't know about their childhood memories, share one of yours!

Alzheimer's cannot take away what had already been. It only transfers responsibility of remembering to those who love the one who is afflicted.
–Natasha in a letter to her grandfather

Newfound Memories

Life Reflection

Look around your home. Do you see pictures to remind you of special times? If someone else looked at those pictures, they just see people. You look at those pictures and you see a wonderful story behind each one.

Every person should have pictures around them that reflect their adventures in life.

Avoid using pictures from the recent past. Because of the person's short-term memory loss, he will not recognize these pictures. One exception to that rule is pictures of grandchildren—everyone loves pictures of babies and kids. But the goal is to find old pictures of the person, including: a picture of him around the age of 18, a picture of his mom and dad, a picture of a childhood pet, or a picture of his children when they were young. I suggest you keep the original pictures and have a copy made to place in a pretty picture frame. Most photo processing centers can make a new photo from a print. That way, your precious old-time photos won't get lost or misplaced. (A person with

Alzheimer's tends to share things, or forget which things are his.)

After getting copies of some photos of your loved one, an important step is writing down the story underneath the picture and identifying the people in the picture. Now anyone who enters their room can give them their history back and get to know them beyond the disease.

> *I would do Dorothy's hair in the morning and within a few hours she would run her fingers continually through her hair until it stood straight up. Needless to say I was a bit frustrated because her hair always looked a bit messy. Later on, her family brought in a picture of her when she was younger. Guess what her hair style was? Pulled straight back into a tight bun. Now I understood that she was doing her hair instead of messing it up.*

When we bring sunshine into the lives of others, we are warmed by it ourselves.
—Barbara Johnson

Newfound Picture

Replacing Priceless Treasures

What looks like junk to you may be a priceless treasure to them full, of fond memories. They should not be robbed of these treasures. If there is something of value, like a tea set, jewelry, wallet, purse, or rock collection, replace it with something that resembles the real item.

> *Mary was in tears, and I asked her why she was crying. She pointed at my wedding ring, and in jumbled words she expressed how her husband would be upset when he found out she had lost her wedding ring. Her husband was no longer living, and her family took her ring, but she could not remember that.*

Another frequent dilemma is whether or not to let the person continue to wear their wedding ring in the chance that it might be lost. First consider these questions:

- Has the person lost a lot of weight so the ring could easily fall off her finger?

- Do you observe the person hiding her ring for safekeeping, which could mean never finding it again?
- Does she give away her ring to a complete stranger?

If you answered, "Yes," to any of these questions, I recommend you keep the ring in a safe place and replace the ring with one that looks a lot like it.

On the flip side, if she is crying and rubbing her hands together in search of her ring, asking about her husband, or able to talk about her ring when someone asks about it, then it is probably better for the person to keep the ring. Many care communities work effortlessly to find lost items. They find them in the strangest places or are unable to find them ever again. Wedding rings are priceless, so seriously consider the outcome.

Another suggestion is to create a memory box—a box that holds significant items that trigger fond memories. In other words, if your mom had dementia, what would you put in a box to let everyone know who she is; her favorite perfume, favorite scarf, jewelry, picture of her sister, love letters from your dad? Then anyone who visits can pick up the box and say, "Alice, this box has your name on it. I wonder what's in here." Then they go through the box together. Other people get to know your mom, and your mom is reminded who she is—even when you're not there.

A daughter shared with me how her dad liked baseball caps, so she ordered a case full of his favorite team. Forty four baseballs caps. When he passed away, she only found two. We looked at each other and said, "Forty two other people are enjoying his baseball cap."

When something you brought in ends up missing, know that you created a moment of joy for two people and not just one. When these things are locked in a closet or in an attic because we are afraid it will get lost, is it bringing joy to anyone? No. Not until you put it in a person's hands. Then the item is priceless.

If a family heirloom is among the items you're considering for a memory box, *REPLACE* it with something that looks similar.

Wallets and purses need to be replaced as well, but be sure to have 10 purses and wallets in the closet for back-up when the original gets lost. Imagine not having your wallet or purse with you. You would feel a little insecure too. Men especially should have a little change in their pocket or a few dollars in their wallet so they feel they are able to pay if the need arises. Yes, it might end up lost, but what is more valuable; the feeling of security or a couple of bucks.

Here are some items you can include:

Purses—plastic cards, handkerchief, compact, lipstick, old checkbook, comb/brush, jewelry, change purse, driver's license, current facility address, and phone number, pictures of grandchildren and other family, pictures of pets.

Wallets—$4, AAA card, military ID card, insurance card, driver's license, active member club card, current facility address and phone number. In addition, handkerchief, pocket change, keys, or a watch on a chain.

Rest assured that it is very normal for purses to be filled with sugar packets, napkins, apples, silverware etc. As long as the purse has weight to it there is value in it.

Be sure to enclose a card with their present address in case the person becomes lost. Another wonderful safety measure is to sign them up with the Safe Return program at the nearest Alzheimer's Association. This enables the community to help bring them home safely. These people are priceless treasures, too.

We too often love things and use people, when we should be using things and loving people.

Newfound Treasure

Habits
of a Lifetime

One of my habits of a lifetime is sleeping with my feather pillow especially when I am traveling. (Yes, I get all kinds of comments in the airport.) If I don't have my feather pillow, I have vivid dreams that someone needs me and I get up and head for the door. By the time I reach the door, I wake up and realize where I am. My friend, Debbie, has to have a fan to fall asleep at night. Try sharing a room with her at a bed-and-breakfast inn. I usually wake up with a scratchy throat and tired eyes while Debbie is refreshed and ready to go. At least she got her sleep.

When someone has Alzheimer's, it is very difficult for them to tell us what their habits of a lifetime are. Grasp the moment now and write down their habits of a lifetime. If they ever lose the ability to communicate, someone else will decide what their wants and wishes are.

The staff told me about a belligerent man who was still cognitive but very uncooperative. I knocked on his door and walked into his room about 9:00 at night. The room was very warm, he was resting on top of his covers with his day clothes on, and there were pictures of horses all over his room. I explained I was just visiting and asked him about the pictures of horses on the wall. He eagerly told me how he was a Texas Ranger and rode all over the United States to compete in rodeos. We had a delightful conversation about him sleeping under the stars and being a bachelor all of his life roaming the countryside. When I left the room, I thought about our conversation. He sleeps on top of his covers with his clothes on because he is accustomed to sleeping under the stars, and his room is really warm because he is used to the heat living in Texas. If he did not have pictures of horses around him, he would essentially lose his sense of identity. With this new information, I was able to understand him. Can you tell me why he was "uncooperative?" He's never been married. Now he has 30 women telling him what to do. Instead of labeling him, staff should have seen this as an opportunity to write down his habits of a lifetime while he is still able to communicate. Imagine how aggressive he would be if he had Alzheimer's and we tried to put him in pajamas and tuck him into bed.

We need to change the way we do assessments of people with dementia. Assessments put too much value into labels. The information we gather from families needs to communicate the important details of a person's history, passions, and interests that help to overcome daily struggles.

It's not so important to know that she is "Catholic," the real value is knowing she carries a rosary in her purse.

It's not so important that he was a "farmer," but the real value comes in knowing he had 725 acres and 100 cattle. That's a fact he may never forget.

It's not so much that she's an "avid reader." The real value comes in knowing she keeps her books under the bed, her favorite book is_____, she likes biographies, and she likes to read around 7 p.m. in her favorite chair with a glass of wine and a bowl of M&M's. The details make all the difference!

Here are some "habits of a lifetime" people have shared with me just for a few smiles….

A lady said she has to eat three walnuts before going to bed. At Christmas time she buys a big bag of walnuts and stocks up for the whole year.

One man had to have three pillows to sleep at night--one between his legs, one between his arms and one at his head (positioned just right.)

A lady had to have a certain pair of socks on her feet to be able to sleep. Well, she and her husband went camping and she had forgotten her socks. So her husband drove 45 minutes out of the way to buy her that specific brand. And, she didn't even have to ask him. (Where did you find that man?)

Another lady slept with a bar of soap between the mattress and the sheet at her feet to fall asleep. Yes, it's a true story. I thought she might be crazy until I shared her story with others. I discovered that more than one person claims it relieves cramps in your legs and relaxes your muscles.

Someone else I met needed a spoonful of peanut butter every night before bedtime.

Another person needed to have the window cracked open, even in the wintertime. The person next to her said she checked her windows before going to bed to make sure they were closed tightly and locked.

A daughter lit up and said, "Now I know why my mom doesn't eat breakfast here! It's because she has always had a cheese sandwich with hot water for breakfast."

We are all made so beautifully different—no two people are the same! And, who is going to think to serve a cheese sandwich with hot water for breakfast! Not me. We are all just around the corner, or maybe a few corners, from needing someone to care for us. If you write down your habits of a lifetime you are more likely to get the kind of care you want and need.

The less we interfere with a person's lifestyle the easier it is for them to adapt to new surroundings.
—Chaplain R.A. Wilcox

Newfound Habits of a Lifetime

Music Does Wonders

If I asked you to sing, "On Top of the World," could you? Probably not, unless you are a big fan of Karen Carpenter. But if I started singing: "I'm on top of the world, looking down on creation and the only explanation I can find..." you probably would be able to sing right along with me .

The same principle works with a person who has dementia. I can almost guarantee if you start singing "Jesus Loves Me" to a person in the late stages of Alzheimer's, you will see some sort of positive response which could be as simple as "comfort" in their eyes. Even if the person is unable to communicate clearly, he can still sing a familiar song. What a gift comfort is. Music is therapy and the results are amazing!

Dorothy usually just shuffled around mumbling noises to herself, but when someone started singing, "I've been working on the railroad" she piped right up and sang every word. When she was singing, she shuffled less, sometimes stood up straighter, and you could see the enjoyment in her face. When staff wanted Doris to cooperate in situations in which she was usually very disagreeable, singing this song usually helped.

If you play music on the radio, be sure it is an "oldies station." I highly recommend getting tapes from the 1900s to 1940s. Voices on the radio might seem like someone is actually talking to them, which could be a good thing or a bad thing. The person's reaction will teach you. But Amos and Andy or a baseball game heard over the radio sure to be a hit.

The look of radios today is unfamiliar, so it helps to buy a replica of the first radios made. Don't be afraid to play the big band peppy music, classical music, or other types of music—just be sure the tone is clear and low in tone. Avoid playing music while asking the person to do a task. For example, don't play music while trying to have a conversation, playing a game, or eating dinner.

Playing music during meals is usually a distraction, rather than a comfort to them. So, turn the music off during the meal. It is difficult for some to eat, let alone eat with noise in the background.

Music is one of the best activities to do over a shift change. The people are less like to see the coming or going of staff because they are having fun singing.

The conventional wisdom that people with dementia have difficulty doing the same thing for a long period of time is not always true. If they like what they are doing and are familiar with the task, they can do the same thing for a long time. So, don't be afraid to sing every day for a full hour. Almost everyone loves music and music triggers good feelings. Music can change a person's mood in the span of a song.

Excerpt from "My Journey into Alzheimer's Disease"

My church was well known for having the best modern church music. I thoroughly enjoyed such music. Now suddenly, I am distracted by this music. Modern music, with its heavy beat produced by guitar, drum, and other dominating instruments, is heard by me only as the beat, accompanied by mingled other sounds. A few minutes of listening to the beat of drums are enough to produce discomfort, even headaches.

God did not leave me comfortless in my need for music to fill my soul. One day I was sorting through my record collection and in that discard process that always comes at the end of a career or the end of life, I found an old George Beverly Shea record. It was one of the first so-called "long play" (33 rpm) records. Out of curiosity, I put it on my phonograph. From that old scratched record came Bev's deep voice singing simple old hymns. I sat back listening, and then realized I actually was enjoying it. This music spoke to me. Eagerly, I picked some of the old records with more old hymns. There came a sense of peace and enjoyment as I listened to these records that I had put away years ago as being merely historical curiosities. Somehow, in the strange thinking of my mind, I had reverted back so that new music was irrelevant, but the old music was spiritually refreshing. I again have music to bless my soul.

You can change a person's mood in a matter of a song.
—Jolene

memory enhanced environments

Newfound Favorite Songs

A Commercial About TV

TV can have negative effects that we blame on Alzheimer's, but is actually a result of watching TV. They cannot separate themselves from what is happening on TV. If someone got shot on TV, the person with dementia might think someone really got shot.

Choose TV programs with happy positive content like musicals, Shirley Temple movies, Lawrence Welk, movies about animals or babies, sports, and possibly some game shows, like "The Price is Right" (but you'd better have prizes in the mail). Even "I Love Lucy" has a story line too detailed to follow and is likely to lose the person's interest.

If they do like certain TV shows, videotape them without the commercials and have them watch the videos over and over.

As I was visiting a care center, I noticed a lady in a wheelchair with a painful look on her face. I knelt in front of her, introduced myself, and asked her if she knew the song "By the Light of the Silvery Moon." I started to sing it, but didn't see a twinkle in her eye. So I tried, "You Are My Sunshine" and she muttered "Ma Ma" now and then. So I knew I triggered a familiar tune.

While I was singing, I heard the roar of a TV in the adjacent room. The music and the words were very harsh and I concluded that this was causing the pain on her face. A nurse came over and was going to give her some pain medication. With a smile on my face and a comforting tone in my voice, I explained that the TV was causing this reaction. I suggested we move her somewhere else before dispensing medication. I continued in a comforting disposition and included the person in the conversation by saying what a lovely lady she was. I didn't want to lose the better mood I created during our short visit. I slowly moved her into the dining room where I said, "Let's sit in front of the window. It is such a lovely day." I commented on a little girl across the street and she replied for the first time plainly and coherently, "Where's her mother?" I assured her that the little girl's mom was watching her out the window. The look of pain vanished from her face.

Story told by many: My mother called me and said she didn't know how she was going to feed all these people in her house and asked if I could come over to help her. I went over to her house, and no one was there, but the TV was on. All those people she was seeing were on TV.

A gentleman was telling his wife about how the place he lived in was dealing drugs. He said drugs were being brought in on the food truck so no one would notice. He was very concerned and wanted his wife to call the police. She went along with his story and said she would take care of it. The next day she met a friend of hers for

*lunch, and her friend told her about a show she watched
the night before about drug dealers smuggling drugs in
on food trucks. What is happening on TV is happening
to a person with dementia.*

Remember, TV for the most part is noise and
usually adds to the person's confusion.

Note: Television volume output can be reduced by
having an 8 ohm register installed in the output wire
to the TV speaker. This in effect doubles the load to the
speaker, and cuts the effective volume in half.

Or you can simply consider this… Ahhhhhhhhh…..
Peace and quiet. A silent gift.

*You and I have learned to tune out what we regard as
background noise and background conversations . . . it is
all "foreground" for her (his mom with Alzheimer's).*
—David Dodson Gray

Newfound Entertainment

Ring, Ring, Ring

Telephones are not recommended in the room of your loved one, because whenever she sees the phone, she is triggered to use it. She doesn't remember calling you just three minutes ago. Therefore, a phone adds stress to your life as well as the person with dementia.

If you have already given the person a phone and want to remove it, one way is to say, "Your phone isn't working correctly, let me get it fixed for you."

Phones ringing behind nurses stations are the source of many negative reactions. When the person hears the phone, she may think it's for her or she is triggered to want to "call home." Mobile phones or pagers that vibrate are a better solution. Locating the phone in a place where they cannot see or hear it is just one way to relieve some unnecessary stress.

We were having a wonderful time singing the old familiar songs and then the phone rang in the background. Three people with dementia got up to answer it. Habit of a lifetime!

However, there are some circumstances where limited use of a phone is comforting to your loved one. It is a good idea to have a backup plan, so when the person gets upset, you are able to give him the illusion of calling "someone." Have a number you can call that has a busy signal so they think someone is talking on the phone, a number that will just ring and ring so they think no one is home, and a number with an answering machine that gives a reassuring message. Sometimes just hearing familiar sounds and voices will convince them that everything is OK for the moment and you will try to call later.

A staff person had a wonderful husband that she would call when a lady wanted to talk to her husband. This lady's husband had passed away but she did not remember that. The staff person's husband would talk with her awhile and reassured her that everything would be OK.

A resident was looking for her dad, especially in the evening. Eventually, the staff figured out that her dad was the one to tuck her in at night. Through the staff's creativity and insight, they made it part of her care plan to call a male nurse working in another area. He would say, "Hi honey. I am working late tonight. I promise to tuck you in when I get home. Sweet dreams, Caroline."

When my mother became upset and anxious I would call one of her friends and they would chit chat as they always had. It changed my mom's mood instantly.

Two ladies were visiting in the back yard and there was a shovel stuck in the ground not far away. One lady sighed and said, "That's as far as he got spading for a garden . . . the worms looked so good he went fishing.

Newfound Ringing

memory enhanced environments

Where's the Outhouse?

Bathroom habits and problems bring up a delicate, particularly humbling, concern for people with Alzheimer's or dementia. Here's an illustration to help you understand the dilemma—and ideas for making this easier.

When Henry wakes up in the middle of the night to use the bathroom he sees two doors—one with a light under it and another door that is dark. He chooses the one with the light. As he walks into the hallway he sees lots of doors and gets confused. In the confusion, he realizes he can't hold it any longer.

One of the main reasons people with dementia are incontinent is because they cannot find the bathroom. They simply cannot remember where it is. A person with dementia only knows what he sees right now. If he doesn't see it, he cannot use it. Verbal reminders alone are not enough because of their short-term memory loss. Changes in the environment can make all the difference.

Suggested Changes

- Make water in toilet blue so men SEE where they are supposed to hit
- Make the bathroom look and feel like a bathroom in your home, with pretty towels, decorative pictures, a picture of an outhouse, and soap bars
- Have a night light on in the bathroom. People with dementia walk where they are able to see
- Leave the bathroom door open so they can see the toilet. They need to see the toilet to know that is the bathroom
- Replace the toilet seat with a color different than the floor color
- Paint the wall behind the toilet a midrange color so the toilet stands out from the wall
- Paint the door to look like an outhouse door
- Paint a half moon on the door (outhouse symbol)
- Paint the bathroom door a different color from the other doors and adjacent wall. Then you can easily say, "It is the white door over there." A person with dementia keeps color definition far into the disease. The bathroom doors should be a color that is different than the bedroom doors
- Place the toilet paper in direct view

Is there a mirror in the bathroom? Yes, of course. Every bathroom has a mirror, right? For a person with dementia, a large mirror in the bathroom might present some problems. Because the person doesn't recognize his own reflection when he walks in the bathroom, he may not want to use it. His perception might be that a stranger is in the bathroom. If the mirror is large and square, it may seem like someone is peeking through the window (mirror) at him.

Also try using their everyday bathroom terms. "It's time to use the outhouse, privy, lavatory, etc.?" They may never have called it a toilet or bathroom so they don't understand what you are saying.

Bathroom clichés

Often, a person with dementia is accustomed to a particular cliché, rather than directly communicating his need to use the bathroom. Here are some common clichés:

"I gotta see a man about the horse."

"I have to shake the rattle snake."

"I need a duck."

"I need to water the bushes/trees."

"I gotta see Mrs. Jones."

"I gotta go pee pee in the teepee."

"Where's the water trough?"

"Where's the privy?"

"Where's the john?"

"I need to find the latrine."

"I gotta shake the dew drops off the lily pad."

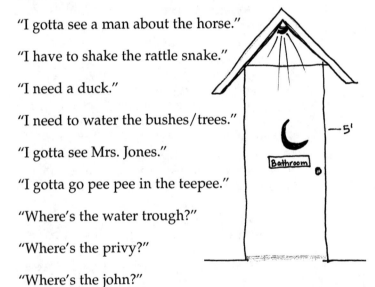

It could be as discreet as, "I need to take a walk." Or, he may only remember how to say bathroom in his native language, if he immigrated to the United States as a youth.

A lady would stand at the door that goes outside and say, "Let me out! Let me out!" She was automatically labeled as an "elopement risk." Someone eventually figured out that when she did this, she actually needed to use the bathroom. In her mind the outhouse was outside! So now when she goes to the door the staff members say, "The outhouse is over here."

There was a gentleman who said when he needed to use the bathroom, "Gotta take a shit." You'd probably like to scold him but you won't change him. Instead of seeing this as a bad word, see it as a treasure. When he loses the ability to communicate, you know the word to use to possibly trigger him to use the bathroom. Yes, write it down!

There are also many nonverbal cues to indicate when a person needs to use the bathroom.

Other visible indicators:
Leaning to one side
Restless
Wandering
Squirming in their seat
Holding private parts
Fidgeting with their pants

Fixing leaks

Many people ask me how to deter men from urinating in wastepaper baskets, wall heaters, closets, fake trees, and many other objects. First, think about little boys (and big boys). Little boys go to the bathroom wherever they are standing. Understand that the wastepaper basket might look like a urinal and the water heater may be perceived as a water trough. The fake tree, of course, seems to be a real one. So I say, the more trees the better. At least they hit something and the tree can be replaced easier than the carpet. It is very difficult to catch men before they urinate, so simply change your mind and start placing wastepaper baskets everywhere. At least it covers the leaks, so to speak. Avoid installing wall heaters, if at all possible, or purchase a plastic cover.

Here is one creative solution to help a man use the bathroom. Hang girly posters in the bathroom. What man doesn't like to linger where there are girly posters? One lady, who grew weary of cleaning up after accidents, knew that a man liked Marilyn Monroe. So, she placed Marilyn Monroe pictures in the places where she didn't want him to urinate. It worked . . . but I forgot to ask, "Where is he peeing now?" Isn't this fun!

> *There were a couple of gentleman trying to get out the locked door. A nurse's assistant walked by, and without missing a beat said, "Gentlemen, that is the lady's bathroom." The men backed away from the door.*

To make it easier to unbuckle a person's pants to use the bathroom, place their hands on your shoulders and ask if they would help hold you up. Reassure with: "Thank you for holding me up. You sure are so strong," or "Your hands are so warm." In many circumstances, it is effective to distract the person by focusing on something else while you do what you need to.

For many men, it is less intrusive if you stand behind them when unbuckling their pants. This feels more natural to them.

Avoid asking if they need to go to the bathroom because they will naturally answer no. Instead use statements like, "Time to get washed up for dinner." Then when you are in the bathroom, simply say, "Better use the john before we go."

While in the bathroom, practice being quiet and invisible by placing yourself to the side or behind the person. Placing your hand lightly on their shoulder may stop them from getting up and down. Another person may feel more comfortable if you hold his hand and chat a lot of nonsense and laugh with them. Every person is different.

Some days, when "accidents" happen, I have to clean her up, of course. And I can tell she's not very happy with the world at all as she says, "What the hell are you doing?" I reply, "Getting you dressed, sweetie." When I'm finished I say, "There, all pulled up and you're cozy warm. OK." I know that when the cleaning up is over and she's clean (and lovely again) she's forgotten the bad stuff and she'll hold me close and just say, "I love you, honey." We just feel very close and stand there together for a few moments in a calm, happy moment. A moment of joy for sure. The shortness of memory that Alzheimer's brings is, of course, often a godsend.

Most of the time, B.M.'s go into the toilet, and that's a moment of joy for me. My wife is not even aware, however, that she's had a B.M. But I make a big celebration of it and do a little jig in front of her. So we have a laugh, despite her probably thinking that I'm a crazy person! That's the type of moment of joy that is mutual!

—Alan Ross, husband and caregiver

Figure out what their habit of a lifetime or routine is when using the bathroom. Organize a routine so you know when to discreetly remind them it's time to use the bathroom.

Before Edith went to sleep, the caregiver assured her the animals were fed, the house was clean, all the baking was done, and she needed to get her rest. With this simple assurance, she would be dry all night, but if they didn't tell her this story she would be wet every two hours.

Leave them with a content feeling before they nod off. It can make all of the difference.

To affect the quality of the day, that is the highest of arts.
— Henry David Thoreau

Newfound "Bathroom"

It's Saturday Night! Bath Time

Motivate, Motivate, Motivate! Whatever you are having difficulty getting the person to do, be creative and think of a way so they will want to do it. The issue of taking a shower is a big one, and I will address it thoroughly so you understand their distress, and I'll offer solutions to make bath time bearable.

One reason showers are so stressful is because they are unfamiliar. When they were growing up they took baths, not showers. They didn't have running water so the noise from the water can be alarming. They usually washed their hair in the sink so shampooing their hair in the shower and water running over their eyes is an unfamiliar process. If they have a hearing deficit and there is a lot of noise in the bathroom (fan, water running, people talking etc.) it can be very frightening. Because they can't hear you, it is difficult to understand what your purpose is. They may not be able to see the water running down their arm, so they could perceive it to feel like bugs. There may be a justifiable fear of water from a past experience, but they may be unable to communicate it. It might just feel and look cold in the bathroom (stark, hard, white-tiled walls).

Another real issue is that they are extremely private people—people who might have dressed in the closet or in the dark. If they were a part of the holocaust, they might think they are in a gas chamber. Being naked may trigger memories of being molested. I know these aren't pleasant reasons why they don't like showers, but the point is to stop blaming the reactions that occur solely on the disease itself. When we say they do something because of the disease we are essentially giving up on one valuable question. "Why?" Why are they reacting like they do?

The key is to explore the family bathing practices. Once we know why, we either will understand and accept, or we will take the first step to figure out a solution to create change. The goal is to prevent the fear of bathing.

Preserving Modesty

- Sew two towels at the top corners creating a "poncho" to put over the person while in the shower or just put a towel over their lap. When the towels are wet use them to clean the person off. Have a dry poncho ready to put on after the shower/bath to dry them off
- Cut a hole in the middle of an old sheet and use it to cover the person completely while bathing
- Wash one area at a time and then cover the area
- Don't hover over them. If possible, do something else while they are bathing: clean, read a book, or pretend you are looking for something (quietly)
- Acknowledge that you respect their privacy by telling them so or looking away when possible

- Start bathing process by washing safe, less intimidating areas (feet, arms)

Helpful Bathtub Hints

- If the person is still mobile, I recommend using bathtubs because they are more familiar
- Fill the tub 1/3 full before the person is in the room to avoid noise
- For some people bubbles and soft music help them relax
- Give the person control by letting them have their own "stuff" (washcloth, soap, glass, not the shower head)
- Only use a little water because, in this person's generation, he didn't waste any water. If you have to fill the tub, verbally reassure him you are going to reuse water to water the plants when you are finished
- Replicate the "sponge bath" or "spit bath." Fill the sink with water and give the person a washcloth and bar of soap

Helpful Shower Hints

- Instead of shower heads, use a colored pail with two colored glasses and have them help scoop the water out so the person not only sees what is going to happen but they relate this with the familiar "sponge bath"
- Use step-by-step instructions and bathe slowly
- Cover shower head with a washcloth. Often, his skin is very sensitive and the shower's spray may be causing pain or fear
- When washing their hair, hold a washcloth against their forehead so water doesn't get into their eyes. (Better yet, have the person hold the washcloth)

- Have a man hold a warm wash cloth over his face and lean back. This is a familiar position before the barber gave him a shave. Less threatening.

Helpful Environmental Hints

- Make the bathroom look, feel, and smell like a bathroom
- Increase the light level three times the normal level so they don't feel like they are in a darkened room
- Reduce noise, rush, and glare
- Paint the walls a warm soothing color
- Be sure to place a mid-range colored towel over the seat or at the bottom of the tub so the person sees where to sit and the seat is no longer cold. (Refer to white on white information under "Quality Connections")
- Keep the bathroom very warm. We all know they already feel cold, and it's difficult to enjoy anything when you are cold. (Install radiating panels and a warming closet)
- Remove or cover up the mirror with a roller shade, because a person with dementia perceives the mirror as a window and someone (their reflection) peeking in on them
- Place pictures of children taking baths in their direct vision to trigger the bathing experience
- Be sure all the items in the bathroom look like something you would put in your own bathroom. If it is clinical looking or doesn't look like bathroom stuff, it should be removed, covered up with a bathrobe, or placed in a closet
- Try a bidet to clean private areas. It is much less intrusive than your hand
- Find an old barber chair with sink so they can have a familiar experience while washing their hair

More Helpful Hints

- Focus all your attention on the person
- Touch gently. When you get older, the skin becomes paper thin and very sensitive. Washing with a wash cloth may hurt. Use soft towels
- Acknowledge their feelings and use genuine magic words: "I am here if you need me. I understand, we will take it slow, and I will be careful. Can I help with that?"
- Bribe with favorite treat. "After you take a shower, I will get you a big bowl of ice cream."
- Motivate: "Let's get freshened up. It will feel good."
- With businessmen, make an appointment on paper and have him sign his name
- If they absolutely resist, leave and try again later
- Find out their habit of a lifetime concerning showers (i.e.: took shower in the morning or evening, with a soap bar or wash cloth, temperature of water)
- Give a reason why they should take a shower: someone is visiting or there is church the next day
- Find ways to give an "illusion" of control
- Stick to a routine
- "It's Saturday night! You get the first hot tub." (Every night can be Saturday night)
- Wash only what is necessary for good health
- To "kick start" the bathing experience, begin by asking him to wash his face
- Use "please" and "thank you" often
- Your mood affects the person's mood. If you are comfortable giving a bath, he is more likely to be comfortable with you
- Easily use words like, "I'm sorry. I didn't mean to hurt you. I'm sorry, that was my fault."

- Involve the person in the process. "I will wash off this arm, and you wash off your other arm."
- State that you do not know how to give a bath and ask her to show you how
- Distract him from the awkward circumstances of the bath by talking about his favorite subject: fishing, cooking, traveling
- Tell her she is queen for the day
- Sing her favorite song
- Turn your questions around so all he has to say is "yes" or "no" or nothing at all
- Give the bath in bed with a warm towel and "no rinse" soap
- Use a gentle touch and pat dry rather than rub to increase comfort
- Respect the person's right to say "no"
- Do something to end this experience on a positive note: give a backrub with Jergen's lotion, comb hair, apply lipstick, put on his cologne to "wow" the women, tell a joke
- Make spa coupons and say, "This is a special treat for the day."
- Have them bathe a baby doll while you are giving them a bath
- Good guy, bad guy. One caregiver is giving the bath and when the person becomes upset, the other caregiver comes in and tells her to leave. This caregiver becomes the hero and he is more likely to cooperate with the person who saved him.
- Alcohol before, during and after the bath☺

George didn't want to take a shower, and it had been two weeks since his last shower. Staff was at their wit's end with finding a solution, so one of the staff called George on the phone and acted like his wife. She told him they were going to visit friends tonight, and he better get cleaned up. It worked!! He took a shower. Now the next time a better answer might be to have the wife really call and tell him something that will encourage him to take a shower. He is less likely to hit you if he understands the reason why he needs to take a shower.

As they were lowering Therstin into a Jacuzzi he yelled "Pig!! Pig!!" He was a farmer, and thought they were lowering him into boiling water. This is how they would get the skin off pigs.

A lady being encouraged to get into a Jacuzzi stated with much resistance, "I don't want soup! I don't want soup!" The large Jacuzzi was a big pot of boiling soup.

Avoid using hot tubs with a person who has dementia, because the bubbles look like boiling water and could cause tremendous fear! For a person who is not cognitively impaired, a Jacuzzi can be very therapeutic. Note: The best tub I have researched and works for most people with dementia is the Parker tub from ARJO.

Another important point to realize is you are giving them partial showers all through the week. Their hair gets washed at the beauty salon, and we clean their private areas if they are incontinent. All we have left are the legs, chest and arms which may be easily done with a traditional sponge bath. Don't feel like you have to submerge them in water to get them clean.

Our home has a scale in the tub and then we use the excuse that the Dr. needs their weight. It gets them in the tub with less problems. We also get our male nursing assistant to put on a white jacket and he becomes the Dr. who recommends a hot bath for therapy.

—nursing assistant who is a bathing expert

If you work in a care center, try having shower experts. This means choosing staff who are good at giving showers, and their main job is to give showers. This not only creates a familiar shower routine for each resident but seeing a familiar face is comforting. Creating a routine is a powerful tool! The shower experts truly become experts at what they do. Priceless!

A friend of mine told me she was the only one who was able to get this lady to take a shower. I said "How do you do it?" She said, "I really like this lady, and others don't because she can be difficult but I say to her, 'June, if you let me help with your shower I promise to make you beautiful.' And I do make her beautiful by combing her hair and putting on her favorite dress. It's quite simple."

It can be that simple! If you are genuine and show the person you care, she will be more likely to cooperate with you. There is a saying I call having "IT." "IT" is a gift that comes naturally. Some of us are naturally wonderful working with older people. Some of us are naturally wonderful with children. Find your strength and focus on it. You will do amazing things!

A lady resisted taking a bath and one day a staff person found out that if she wore an apron, the bathing experience went much better. I'd bet her mom wore an apron. Yes, you should smile . . . people with aprons on look like warm, friendly moms.

Life is either a daring adventure or nothing. To keep our faces toward change and behave like free spirits in the presence of fate is strength undefeatable.
— Helen Keller

Newfound Bathtime Routine

memory enhanced environments

Suppertime!!!!!

You know how before you get to a baseball game you say to yourself… "I'm not going to eat a hot dog. I'm not going to eat a hot dog." But as soon as you get there and you smell the hot dogs and see people eating them…you have to have a hot dog. Or when you go to the movies and think, "I don't need any snacks." But when you walk through door you have to have some popcorn. It's funny how our sense of smell and the environment triggers the need to eat even when we are not hungry. It holds true for almost all of us no matter if we have a illness or not.

So I challenge you to look at your dining rooms and ask yourself, "Does this environment make people WANT to eat?" Answering the next few questions may help you come to a conclusion. Does this dining room look, feel, and smell like a dining room? Is there china on the wall? Is there an old buffet? Are there pictures of food or pictures you would see in a dining room? Do the tables have tablecloths over them? A person with dementia knows only what he sees. So, he needs to see things that trigger the dining experience.

Since people with dementia cannot handle large spaces, you may need to break up the space to make it feel smaller and look more like home. Some suggestions include a buffet, a partial wall, a hanging quilt, and a wall curtain. Do whatever it takes to break up the room visually and acoustically.

Provide optimum lighting so people are able to see everything clearly. Incorporate visuals that say this is a dining room, like a spoon rack or a shelf for plates and hanging teacups. Incorporate pictures that clearly look like food, like a bowl of fruit or a picture of bread and wine. The picture of a praying man and the praying wife are familiar and also the picture of "The Last Supper." Put them at eye level when they are sitting down. Create a dining room that looks, feels, and smells like a dining room. This may be one of the most powerful changes you can make.

Level of Development

In the middle to late stages of dementia, this person could have the developmental level of a child who is 3, or even younger. When you correlate the development level with a person in your care, you can have the opportunity to come up with some effective solutions.

When my daughter turned 2, I told her she doesn't have to have a "sippy cup" anymore. So I gave her a glass of milk. What was the first thing she did? She poured milk all over her food. When she did that I thought of Thirsten, one of the people I used to care for. Every time Thirsten came to the table, he would pour his milk over his food. I corrected him but did he change? No. Guess who has to change--we do. I wish I would have tried a cup with a lid and straw. My one-year-old can handle a straw. I know what you are thinking. Is that age appropriate? It isn't always about being age appropriate but it's more important to be successful. The other side of the coin would be . . . is milk on his food going to hurt him? No. So, stop correcting him and encourage him to eat. They cannot change; they are doing the best with the abilities they have left. We need to be the ones to change.

As the disease progresses their developmental level regresses. Here are some examples in which developmental level is compared with mealtime.

What would happen if you give a one-year old a plate of food? He would dump it.
Solution: When eating becomes difficult for a person with dementia offer one item of food at a time in separate bowls.

What would happen if you put salt and pepper shakers, three glasses of beverages, three utensils, and a plate of food in front of toddlers? They would play with them.
Solution: If the person is unable to focus on the meal reduce the number of items in front of the person to a minimum. One glass and one utensil.

Do your kids come to the table, sit down, and not get up through the whole meal? No.
Solution: Allow people with dementia to eat on the run.

Do your kids eat food they don't like no matter how much you persuade them? No.
Solution: Take the time to figure out what foods the individual likes and dislikes.

What would your kids be saying if you didn't have any snacks around?   I'm hungry.

Solution: Having snacks available is just as important as meals themselves.

What finger foods do our kids like?

Answer: Cheese slices, sandwiches (cut up into four and take the crust off because they don't like anything hard…sound familiar?), oranges, apples (peeled of course), Jell-O jigglers, dry cereal, raisins, hot dogs sliced long ways, Nutri-Grain bites, little muffins (big ones cause a mess), toast with jam or cinnamon and sugar, pancakes (rolled up with sugar), grapes, carrot sticks (boil to soften), broccoli sticks (boiled), cauliflower sticks (boiled), cold beans from a can (yes my kids and I love those to munch on), cherry tomatoes, strawberries, French toast, cookies, ice cream and the list goes on forever. Think of what your kids like and I'd bet a person with dementia would like it too.

Do children get overwhelmed by large portions?   Yes.

Answer: People have been taught to clean their plates. Therefore, petite ladies get overwhelmed by too much food. Reduce the size of the plate and the portions so it looks like an amount they can eat. Care communities simply need to get a doctor's orders to make this change. This change will also reduce the amount of food wasted.

> *Alice was a petite lady and for the longest time she would come to the table, bang her walker, and walk away. We finally figured out she didn't want a large amount of food so we served her food on a smaller plate with teaspoon size portions and she sat down and ate. It was that simple.*

You get the idea…now have some fun and try it. I was fortunate enough to be able to have kids at home so I could try things out on them first before I tried it with a person with dementia.

Here are some more helpful hints to create an enhanced dining experience.

Before Meals

- Carry a plate of food around and talk in detail how yummy it is and that it is "dinner time" or "supper time!"
- Tearing lettuce, snapping beans, taking the shell off of hard boiled eggs, buttering bread, shucking corn, peeling potatoes, pouring beverages. Get their taste buds going by working with food before meals
- While walking a person to the dining room talk about favorite foods. "We are having fried chicken." or "Do you like apple pie?"
- "Hey let's go for a walk. Look, we made it just in time for lunch."
- Let the men escort you to dinner. Avoid pulling on their arms
- While waiting for the meal (social time) have bread and butter to nibble on. (Who would we be if we couldn't nibble?)
- Offer bacon strips or lemon drops before meals to increase saliva. Saliva is necessary in order to "taste" food. A "sour" or strong taste will stimulate saliva flow
- Warm up wet washcloths in the microwave and hand them to people to "wash up." Nothing feels better than a warm washcloth over your face

Incorporate Traditions

- "Would you help me set the tables?" Give the person—one at a time—the place mats, glasses, napkins, silverware. If they only stack the placemats, and put glasses in a row and then start folding napkins, reply "Thank you for all of your help. It looks great! Why not relax and dinner will be ready in 10 minutes." Even though they may not set the table correctly they have helped you to the best of their ability. Correcting how they have helped will only cause frustration
- Encourage them to "get washed up for dinner."
- Have a bell or triangle and ring while saying "dinner time!"
- Ask someone to bless this meal. Another option is to pray together "Be Present at Our Table Lord" or "Come Lord Jesus." Many people from their generation have been taught not to eat until someone prays
- Before the noon meal turn on the radio and listen to the farm report
- Instead of saying it's time for a snack, say it is time for "coffee." Coffee is a trigger word

> *There was a lady who would not eat in the dining room. Staff members learned that she was a farmer's wife and her tradition was to feed the men first and she would then eat in the kitchen by herself.*

Provide Structured Seating

- Give a reason for a person to sit a certain place and absolutely avoid telling a person, "You have to sit here" Instead say, "Joe, why not sit over here by Fred. He's a smart business man just like you."
- Draw a seating arrangement so people with the same functioning level are sitting together

- If a person is disruptive or has distasteful eating habits you could have them sit in a place visually away from the majority of people.

I was asked to observe the dining experience and offer suggestions on how to stop this certain lady from yelling at mealtimes and prevent another gentleman from getting up and down frequently. As I approached the dining room, I saw that there were approximately 50 people eating at the same time in a large open space. Trays were clanging, music blaring, and staff members were walking around the room. I knew right away I could not do anything with this space to stop the negative reactions of these certain people. I asked them to show me other places close to the dining room. We came upon a wonderful small room that had a kitchenette and simple table. They told me this was reserved for families to visit and eat. My question, "Do the families live here?" Eating is one of the last enjoyments people with dementia have on a regular basis. The first priority should always be the people who live there. People will eat better in a comfortable, small, quiet, dining room. They are now using that space for people who have difficulty eating with lots of people or who are disruptive. It was a WIN/WIN situation for all. By the way, the music in the background was a request from one gentleman. Music during mealtimes is simply extra noise. My philosophy is to make decisions which are in favor of the majority, not the minority.

During Meals

- Create a social atmosphere by introducing people to one another, starting conversations, and eating with them. Pretend as though you were inviting this person into your home and introducing him to your family

- Turn off the TV! Eliminate noise any way you can
- Allow the person to take as much time as needed to eat their meal. How would anyone respond if rushed through a meal?
- Sit down, and eat with the person with dementia. This practice not only creates a normal dining experience, but you are more likely to focus your attention on the person rather than talking with friends or coworkers
- Cut meats and other items before serving food. Do not cut food in front of the person because this makes the food less appealing
- Don't bring the person to the table until the food is ready. No one likes to wait
- If the person is in a wheelchair, help them into a dining room chair. Wheelchairs are not usually at the proper height for eating
- Ensure the person is sitting up as straight as possible
- Before you push the person's chair in ask his permission so he isn't startled by unexpected movement
- Be sure there is a contrast between the table and the plate

Reasons Why They May Not Be Eating

- You haven't sat down yet. It would be rude to eat before everyone has been seated
- The plate is too big with too much food (ladies especially)
- They are unable to see food directly in front of them. Find out where their line of sight is by putting their favorite food in colored bowl and moving it around until they reach for it

- They cannot see white on white. If a plate is white and potatoes, eggs, noodles, and chicken are white, they may not be able to see them. Put gravy or syrup over everything, and serve eggs sunny side up
- The person cannot start the motion of eating, so place your hand over their hand and assist in giving two bites
- There is too much noise around them so they are unable to focus on eating
- Their dentures are uncomfortable or the food is too hard
- They have pain or discomfort
- They don't like the taste of the food or the food is unfamiliar to them
- Be sure table height is appropriate to chair height. Elbows need to be above the table
- They cannot open juice containers or aren't familiar with them so don't know what they are for
- There are too many choices. Offer one item at a time in separate bowls and wait until they are finished before you give them the next item

I took my little boy to visit a memory care home. The staff thought this would be a great opportunity to get a certain lady to come out of her room to eat because she loved kids. She was given a bowl of salad and began eating with us. She was doing just fine and we were having a lovely time talking. Soon after a staff person came over and moved her salad (which she had not finished) to the side and set down her plate of food. Next thing I know, she dumped her salad onto her plate of food, stuck her fork in the food and left the table. Offer one item at a time and wait until they are finished before you give them the next item.

For Assisted Diners (Not Feeders)
- Tell the person what you are giving them
- Serve food in small portions
- SLOW DOWN!!
- Normalize the eating experience by socializing like you do while eating with friends
- Don't make the person eat something they don't like
- TALK WITH A SOOTHING TONE OF VOICE
- Don't talk about the person as if she weren't there
- Reduce noise, especially talking among staff
- Rub the person's throat to trigger swallowing
- Place food or spoon on lower lip to trigger lip closure
- Place cup on lower lip, making sure the tongue is under the edge
- Allow the person to swallow food completely before giving her another bite
- Keep trying something different until you find what works
- Leave the spoon in their mouth so they grab for it and start the eating process independently
- Start with ice cream. It triggers the swallowing experience.

After Meals
- Ask them to help clean up after meals: moving chairs, wiping off place mats, picking up plates, wiping off tables. For those people who aren't mobile, have them clean place mats, while sitting at the table
- Pass around wipes so people can wash their own face and hands. Or take the individuals to the bathroom and cue them to wash their hands and face

- Lay residents down for a nap about 45 minutes after they eat. Fatigue is one of the main causes of negative behaviors. (Refer to "Get Your Zzz's")

Helpful Hints
- Do whatever it takes to dispense medications before or after meals. This will reduce noise and assist in creating a normal dining experience
- Ice cream stimulates swallowing
- Popcorn poppers and bread makers are a must to create a yummy aroma
- Serve soup in a coffee cup; it's easier then using a spoon
- Figure out what their favorite foods are and make food look like that. Everything looks like a pie... quiche!
- Prunes taste better when they are warmed up
- Wear an apron while serving food. (Better yet, department heads, wear aprons and walk around creating a social atmosphere. You would be amazed at what kind of relationships you would build and the understanding you would gain about each person.)
- Serve liquids in a fountain cup with a lid and a straw. Reduces spills and retain ability to sip through a straw

A lady loved ice cream cones so her food was mashed up and put in a cone. Potatoes were vanilla ice cream and carrots were sherbet.

A wife was telling me about her husband who just had a stroke and how he wasn't eating. So one day, she brought him two pieces of fried chicken and he ate it! The next day she brought him four pieces of fried chicken and he ate it all! Again, she brought him six pieces of fried chicken and he ate it! Is it hurting him? No!!! Fried chicken is a familiar food and he can eat with his fingers instead of a spoon.

When a person wants to pay for the food or he says he doesn't have any money to pay for the food, here are the two best answers I've heard: "You have worked hard all your life. This is Uncle Sam's way of paying you back."

Or "The church ladies have made a wonderful meal for all of you." It would be rude of them to turn down food that ladies worked so hard to prepare. Not only that, it's free!

I learned early on that setting the table is so much more than just laying down knives and forks. It is creating a setting for food and conversation, setting a mood and an aura that lingers long after what was served and who said what was forgotten.

—Peri Wolfman

Newfound Dining Experience

Sundowning

My theory on Sundowning is they have *had it* by 3 p.m. They are tired, stressed to the max and just can't do it anymore. So, the next time you put the cereal in the refrigerator and the milk in the cupboard and yell at your husband, you are "sundowning." We have simply labeled it for them because they have a disease. Don't get me wrong, I am not saying emotions and the ability to function don't change around 3 p.m. I simply believe a cause exists for why they do what they do.

Maybe an individual had too much stimulation. Maybe she is restless because she sat all morning. Maybe she feels the need to go home because this is the time of day when her kids would be home, or she needs to start cooking supper. Maybe she has been corrected all day. Maybe her normal daily routine has been interrupted. Maybe you are tired and are less patient with her today. Whatever the reason, I believe there is a reason.

I recommend three changes to make the day move along smoothly. First of all, do whatever it takes to start the morning on the right foot. If that means allotting more time for her to get dressed and groomed, letting her sleep in, or doing her hair—do what needs to be done. If she gets to start the day feeling well and looking good, she will play better throughout the day. The morning is a good time for you to have someone help out so you can start your morning off on the right foot, too.

Next, be sure the person gets at least one nap during the day. But if you ask, "Do you want to take a nap?' Her answer will be no, because in her generation many of them did not take naps.

Instead, sit down with her and slowly read a story in a deep monotone voice, and it kind of sounds like this: "Along came a big yellow lab and he walked up to the front porch and laid down under the warm sun. Yawn. It was such a lovely day. Yawn. It felt good to bask in the warm breeze. Yawn. Then a small gray kitty came out of the barn, waddled across the yard, and up to the front porch. Yawn. The little gray kitty snuggled up next to a big yellow lab and fell sound asleep. Yawn. It was a hot, hot, hot day . . . "

When you look up and find 10 or 12 people sleeping, I want you to go 'Yeeah!!!!!!' Not aloud, of course, but give yourself silent affirmation because you have just given her the cat nap she needs to get through the afternoon. Fatigue is a major cause of many of the negative reactions that occur later in the day, including sundowning.

Simply think to yourself what activity have I done that has put everyone to sleep and do that after lunch. (church music, reading scripture, church sermon on TV)

Finally, prior to the time the person becomes most anxious, I want you to do something the person loves. While I was an activity person, the one thing I could always count on to get through the confusion of shift change was singing. A half an hour before the first shift was over, I would start to sing the old familiar tunes and we would continue to sing until the second shift was in place.

If you don't find something to capture an individual's attention, he is simply watching the coming and going of all these people who are saying, "Goodbye!" or "I gotta go get my kids." For a person with dementia, shift change will bring out a variety of extreme emotions. She will want to go home with you, she will want to call her kids, repetition will increase, wandering will increase, and anxiety will increase.

When leaving your shift, give the people a place where they don't want to go with you such as, "I have to use the bathroom." "I have to go to work." "I have to go to the dentist."

We know the development level of a person with dementia is usually around a three-year-old child. Imagine if you dropped your preschooler off at preschool and they didn't have any structure or routine but just open gym all day long. How would they be when you picked them up at 3:30. Two boys fighting. Little girl sleeping in the corner. Another girl hanging on the adult saying, "I want my mom. I want to go home."

Does this remind you of any other environment? A dementia care community possibly that doesn't have any structure or routine set up for the day? People with dementia need to keep busy. When children aren't busy, what do they get into? Trouble.

If your child didn't get a nap, how would they be late afternoon? More than cranky!

If you want less sundowning you need to provide structure and routine throughout the day, so we can ALL enjoy a better day.

People with dementia don't operate by a thought process. They operate by how they feel.

—Jolene

Newfound Sun

Labeling

Words matter. What we choose to say about any given topic impacts people's opinions and feelings in positive or negative ways. This proves just as true for the way we communicate about people with Alzheimer's, and the things they do every day.

When I tell you the person is "wandering," how do you feel about what they are doing? Positive or negative? But when I say the person is 96, and still walking up and down the hall, how do you feel? Positive or negative?

When I say to you, a lady is "hoarding" stuff in her room, how do you feel? Positive or negative? But when I say she feels more secure when she is surrounded by items that she can ration, how do you feel about what she is doing?

When I say to you, a man is "combative", how do you feel about him? However, when I say, "He felt threatened by what someone did," how do you respond? With compassion. See the difference?

In healthcare we like to label people with dementia or blame their actions with Alzheimer's terminology. Do we (cognitive people) get labeled as an "elopement risk" when we walk through a door? No. What do we all do with doors? Go through them. For some reason, when someone gets dementia we label them because they want to use a door.

When we use these terms in public (agitated, combative, exit seekers, sundowning), how are we affecting how society feels and thinks about Alzheimer's? Afraid, negative, these people are scary. For those of us who have worked with people who have Alzheimer's, are they scary monsters? Absolutely not...they are more likely to be the funniest person you have ever met with quick one liners. I, personally, would rather hang out with people who have dementia than cognitive people.

Take the challenge...change your language and we may just change the way society thinks about Alzheimer's.

> *I will never forget a daughter in tears telling me how she called a community to check to see how her mom was doing. The lady on the other end of the phone checked her charts and said, "Your mom hasn't been naughty today."*

How would *you* feel if I said to *you*, "Your mom is combative?" Let's be very careful and courteous about what we say. That's the right thing to do. When we choose our words wisely, we have shown compassion.

What goes into the mind, comes out in a life.

Newfound Language

Get Your Zzz's

No matter whether they have dementia or not, as people get older their sleeping patterns change. They might go to bed at 8:00, get up at 1:00, stay up for a couple of hours, go back to sleep until 6:00, and then take two naps during the day.

Fragmented sleeping is an issue which evolves with age. Fatigue is a major cause of the many challenges we face. In the past, we have resorted to keeping people up all day, thinking they will sleep better at night. But this usually backfires and adds great fatigue during the day. Be sure your loved one gets at least one nap a day. (Caregivers, you could use that nap, too!)

A gentleman who was not able to sleep became disoriented, incoherent, and lethargic. They warmed up a towel and put a sock filled with rice into the microwave. They placed the towel over his head and the sock over his shoulders and sat with him. He finally fell asleep. Do you know, the next day he was a different man. He joined in discussion, laughed and made jokes. It was a night-and-day difference when he got his much needed rest.

The staff talked about a gentleman who they would put into bed and within minutes he was up wandering around again. They asked his wife what his evening routine was. The wife said he never wore pajamas, he always slept in the nude. Staff had been putting pajama clothes on him, which to him meant that it was time to get up and start the day.

Any older person, whether he has dementia or not, should be allowed to wake up at his or her own time. How would it be if you woke up a child in the morning before it was time, or imagine a child who didn't get a nap? Not a pretty sight! It is the same for someone with dementia. If someone woke me up before 7:30, I would be agitated and disoriented, too. We all have different needs. Some of us are night owls and some of us are morning people. Whatever the case, you are fighting a losing battle to try to change someone's timetable. This is their last trip. May we allow them to continue to be who they are?

The trouble with being on your feet all day, walking from one end of the building to the other, is that your legs get tired as well as the rest of your body. Caregivers know that. Add to that, the fact that you are 90, and you would really get tired

We knew it was time for Sara to take an afternoon nap long before she was willing to give in to lying down. The aides took turns walking Sara to her room, helped her get her feet on the bed, covered her up and left the room. A few feet down the hall, we'd hear the shuffle of her short, choppy steps, look back and there was Sara, gaining on us. The time we spent trying to get her to lie down was wasted. Her attitude became more cranky with each trip back to her room until finally she refused to go with us. All the while, Sara was slowing down from hours of roaming the halls, and we worried that she would fall.

One afternoon, I took Sara by the hand and asked her to come for a walk with me. Of course, we ended up in her room. I sat her down on the bed, helped her get her feet up, covered her up and left the room just as we had done every other day, and like every other day, I looked back to find Sara was right behind me.

Again, I took her back to her room to repeat putting her in bed. "You need to lay down for a nap. Aren't you tired, Sara?"

"Yes," she admitted.

"Well, why won't you stay in bed then and take a nap?"

"Because I want you to stay here with me." Sara's plaintive voice held an unspoken plea.

There we had it. She was lonely and fearful of being left in that empty room by herself. She was in a large place where the sounds of doors banging, a variety of voices, and loud alarms seemed endless. In her confusion, she feared everything around her and what she heard. Now I understood why she kept following us out of the room.

What did I do? I promised that I would stay with her. I pulled up a chair, sat down by her bed and held her hand. Fighting sleep for a few minutes, Sara peeked over at me from slit eyelids to make sure I was still there until finally her hand went limp in mine, and she breathed deeply in a sound sleep. Then I slipped out of the room.

Taking the time to sit by her bedside to give her peace of mind took far less time than walking her back to her room on those repeated trips. When she woke up rested and ready for the evening meal, Sara wasn't upset that

I hadn't stayed with her during the nap, because she had Alzheimer's, and she didn't remember that I had promised to stay.

—Fay Risner

The key is to leave someone with a peaceful feeling before they fall asleep. Might I even suggest to lie down with someone for a few minutes to give them the comfort and warmth they need to fall asleep. (Look out . . . you may fall asleep yourself.)

An elderly man was afraid to go to sleep at night. The staff person set an empty chair beside his bed each night and said, "This chair is for Jesus. He will stay here all night and watch you while you sleep." Months later, when the man passed away in his bed, his hand had reached out to Jesus. His hand was laying on the empty chair.

Suggestions to help get their Zzz's

- Expose them to sunlight- there is vitamin D in the sun rays to help us sleep better
- Keep people physically active during the day (See the "Walking, Walking Walking" chapter)
- Establish a calming evening routine
- With a little research, you can find foods to eat that help us sleep better at night
- Eliminate stimulating activities after 7:00 p.m.
- Put on an extra blanket an hour after the person has fallen asleep to keep them warm. Being cold is one reason why they don't sleep well. Remember this disease makes them colder than cold
- If the person is used to sleeping with someone else, get a body pillow and spray it with the cologne or perfume of the other person

- Read poetry, rhymes, or sing quiet songs as an evening activity. A steady beat or rhythm is like a lullaby at night
- Use white noise. It is a little machine that makes a subtle noise that is soothing to fall asleep to
- Fulfill habits of a lifetime—sleeping with a feather pillow, sleeping with the fan on, sleeping with a night light, or ensuring that the room is pitch dark
- Allow the person to sleep in his own bed, no matter where they move. (Isn't that what you would want?)
- A common reason why people wake up in the middle of the night is to use the bathroom, but they are unable to tell you, so it should be the first thing you ask
- Let the person wake up on their own in the morning
- Walking, walking, walking

A lady would not calm down. Pacing up and down the hall. The hair dresser just so happened to stop by and didn't understand. This same lady was always relaxed when getting her hair done. So she walked the lady into her beauty shop and set her under the hair dryer. The only comment made was, "And the world goes away." Then she nodded off. What is in her room today? A hair dryer. How many other ladies would love for the world to go away.

My grandma would fight to get undressed for bed at night because she was convinced someone was going to steal her left shoe. (We still haven't figured out why it was only her left shoe.) My mom stepped in and requested to let her keep her shoes on until she fell asleep. The battle was resolved. Choose your battles wisely.

—Renae Smothers

In the case where spouses are care providers, giving medication to the person with dementia may help both the spouse and the person with dementia get their much-needed sleep. You may want to consult with your family doctor about this issue. A glass of wine or shot of whiskey may be the best medication in the cupboard.

My daughter shared with me that when her little boy was a baby, he would have crying fits that seemed to have no discernable cause. To soothe him, she would wrap him in a blanket and then place her arms around him, holding him gently along his sides.

I decided to try this with a resident at work who frequently becomes anxious, tearful, and complains of pain. I had her cross her arms over her chest, hugging herself, then I tucked a soft blanket around her. Next, I sat on a stool in front of her, placing my arms along the sides of her thighs. We didn't talk; we just sat quietly. She began to visibly relax and was then able to fall asleep.

—Gretchen Mellberg

"That we are not much sicker and much madder than we are is due exclusively to that most blessed and blessing of all natural graces, sleep."
—Aldous Huxley

Newfound Zzz's

Enhanced Moments

Touch many . . .
radiate your warmth
                    —*Jolene Brackey*

Simple Pleasures

Think back to when you were a child and all the simple pleasures you found: watching ants build their house, lying under the stars, running outside in the rain, licking a lollipop, eating ice cream, walking through tall grass, finding a new flower, searching for beautiful rocks—simple pleasures we need to relive again.

A simple pleasure for an older person might be those things, and it might be having their hair combed slowly, getting a back rub, feeling lotion rubbed into their hands, receiving flowers, getting their teeth brushed gently, eating with a friend—the list is endless.

Focus on simple pleasures—it's not spending hours organizing a big party or buying the person a whole new wardrobe. It's all about fulfilling basic needs to the fullest. It's as simple as cleaning someone's glasses. You will be amazed by the gratitude you receive because now they can see better.

It's truly a gift, especially in the last stages of Alzheimer's, to understand the importance of simple pleasures.

This is a story my grandma wrote while in a nursing home watching a bird outside her window. In the beginning it doesn't make perfect sense but read on because it is a beautiful story. You will hear so much more if you take the time to listen to a person with dementia.

No one would think I have to see my articles to write and I studied long to find something to write about. Then about a block away a drama took place way up in a tall tree… "Unheard Chirp" by Nellie Larson. Two birds appeared, both looking very tired. The older bird started nest building while little Peter sat in another tree feeling very neglected. But mother was so busy building it didn't matter. At last the nest was finished and the mother bird laid an egg. The nest was lined with the soft down of her breast. Day after day she sat. It seemed such a long time. Each day she turned the egg. At last she heard a peep and a tiny hole appeared. Then a bigger one. Mother helped and soon the little fellow was out and drying nicely. Mother was so proud of him as he dried and turned a nice yellow, soft down. The End.

> *Little things mean everything.*
> — Samuel Johnson

Newfound Simple Pleasures

You've Got Mail!

Everyone has a lifetime of receiving mail. Who would you be without your mail? It's a way of daily connecting with the outside world and knowing what is going on around you. Even if you feel uncomfortable visiting someone with Alzheimer's, a wonderful gift you can always give is mail.

Together, you and your loved one can write a card and send it out to one of her friends or family. Ask her what she would like to say and encourage her to sign her name at the bottom. People with dementia are able to write their signature far into the disease. What joy a daughter would feel to receive a birthday card from her mom as she always had before Alzheimer's.

Send a magazine subscription to them on a subject they enjoy! Because they usually lose the ability to read, find magazines with lots of distinct clear pictures.

We all love to receive packages in the mail, so send thoughtful simple gifts: pretty jewelry, candy, poems, perfume, fishing lures, and other fun things.

A care center can "create" mail by recycling unwanted junk mail, magazines, or newspapers. If you live near a small town, order the community newspaper. I don't recommend subscribing to a city paper that has bad news. Today's news can be extremely scary and confusing.

The greatest and most simple mail is a card. Get cards that say, "Thinking about you" or "You are a special friend" or "Hello."

As I was finishing up a presentation to a retirement community, a lady came up to me and told me of a friend she had known since childhood. She talked about how they lived together for 10 years and they continued to write even though they were miles apart. She found out that her friend had Alzheimer's and her friend stopped writing. She asked me if it would do any good to continue to write, even though she didn't get any letters back. "Of course," I said, "....Yes you must continue to write and give back the memories from long ago." I was fortunate enough to meet this lady again and she shared with me her wonderful story.

"I wrote long letters to my friend, telling her of our funny moments, our adventurous moments, and our quiet moments from long ago. I also sent her pictures that we had taken together in our younger days. I did not hear back from her, but her daughters called me and said the letters and pictures brought laughter, tears, and joy. The daughters heard stories they never knew about their mom and they read the letters over and over again. I was filled with such joy to know I brought moments of joy to my dear friend."

There are countless stories of how people with Alzheimer's find these cards every day and read them as if it were the first time. Smile. Anyone can give this moment of joy. Everyone can pop something in the mail.

Two men, both seriously ill, occupied the same hospital room. One man was allowed to sit up in the bed for an hour each afternoon to help drain the fluid from his lungs. His bed was next to the room's only window. The other man had to spend all his time flat on his back. The men talked for hours on end. And every afternoon, when the man in the bed by the window could sit up, he would pass the time by describing to his roommate all the things he could see outside. The man in the other bed began to live for those one-hour periods where his world would be broadened through these mental pictures of the world outside. The window overlooked a park with a lovely lake filled with ducks and swans, children playing, young lovers walking. The man by the window described all of this in exquisite detail, so the other man could see it in his mind's eye. Days and weeks passed. One morning, the nurse arrived only to find the lifeless body of the man by the window, who had died peacefully in his sleep. The other man was saddened. As soon as it seemed appropriate, the other man asked if he could be moved next to the window and the nurse was happy to make the switch. Slowly, painfully, he propped himself up on one elbow to take his first look at the world outside. Finally, he would have the joy of seeing it for himself. He strained to slowly turn to look out the window beside the bed. It faced a blank wall. The man asked the nurse what could have compelled his roommate who had described such wonderful things outside this window. The nurse responded that the man was blind and could not even see the wall. She said, "Perhaps he just wanted to encourage you."

—Unknown

That is precisely what a letter can do—encourage someone.

You choose . . . be a drop of rain or a ray of sunshine
—Unknown

Newfound Message to Send

"Help me."

Whatever your task may be, ask the person to help you. Human beings possess an innate desire to feel needed. Encouraging them to be responsible for the home might make it seem more like "home".

I asked two ladies to help me set the table. They lined up the glasses on one table, stacked place mats here and there, plates were randomly placed on the tables and one of the ladies started folding the napkins. I could have corrected them and said, "That's not where the glasses go. Glasses go above the plates." But instead I said, "Oh thanks so much for all your help. Why not relax in the living room while I finish dinner. I'll call you when it's ready." After they left, I easily set the tables the right way. Not only did they "help me" but they were a part of the meal preparation, which triggers the appetite. If you are concerned about sanitation, purchase an extra set of dishes at a thrift store, just for the seniors so they can help rinse and wash dishes, too.

Have them help you clean a closet, cut out coupons, move boxes, make beds, sweep the patio, rake leaves, hang clothes, wipe furniture, wash dishes, fold laundry, peel oranges, sort cards, roll yarn, stack wood, shell corn to feed the squirrels, water the garden, snap beans, clean strawberries, polish and sort silverware, crack peanuts, tear lettuce for a salad, butter bread, and the list goes on forever.

Create things for them to do even if it doesn't need to be done. The key is to choose something they have done frequently in the past. And guess what—you can offer the same projects every day because they don't remember they did it the day before. One of my favorites was rolling up yarn. Once a week, I would pull out a box of yarn, unroll it and bring it into the living room and say, "I found this in the closet, and it's a mess. Would you help me roll this yarn up?" Men helped, too, because they liked to help the ladies.

Simplify, simplify, simplify and then let go of expectations. A good example of this is if you asked them to help you weed the garden, and they pull up a few flowers. Stop and think, "Who cares?" The flowers only cost pennies. The point is, they get to experience gardening—something they may have always enjoyed doing. Not only are you providing exercise and relieving stress, you are allowing the person to feel needed and wanted. No expectations attached!

Better yet . . . just plant weeds.

Newfound Jobs They Like To Help With

When In Doubt . . . Laugh

The time to laugh is when we don't have time to laugh
— Argus Poster

If the person fills the refrigerator with stuffed animals or hides fruit all over the house...laugh and continually remind yourself "So what!!" Laughing enhances our sense of well-being, reduces stress, and improves our ability to survive a crisis. Physically, it increases circulation, reduces blood pressure, promotes brain functioning, relaxes muscles, reduces pain by increasing endorphins in the bloodstream, and stimulates the thymus gland, which improves the immune system.

I know that information wasn't funny like you thought this section would be, but hopefully it helps you understand the power of laughter. If you can't find anything to laugh about, just start laughing about nothing until you are laughing at yourself. If you laugh a lot, when you are older all your wrinkles will be in the right places!

If you haven't noticed, people with dementia can make incredibly witty and funny comments. I used to keep a small book in which I wrote down the funny things they did and said. This book was read by staff, and I feel it increased morale.

Another idea is to surround yourself with things that make you laugh: jokes, funny cards, comic strips, fun "stuff." Arrive at someone's bedside with a joke instead of complaining about your day.

Whatever it takes to laugh "Do it!" You will be healthier for it and so will the people around you because laughing is contagious.

A caregiver who liked to tell jokes, told me that when she told jokes to people with dementia they would roar with laughter, even if they didn't understand. It was all about the inflection in her voice and beginning the joke with a familiar phrase, such as "Did you hear about the one . . ."

An activity person was having a discussion group with people who had dementia. One of them walked into the room and said loudly, "Oh, you think you're cute, but I know better. I saw you on the street downtown. You're a nasty hooker." Obviously this could have been a very sticky situation, and everyone was wide eyed waiting for a reaction. The activity person just started laughing and soon everyone began to laugh. Eventually they forgot why they were laughing. The person could have been watching a TV show with hookers on it and felt hookers were in the building. The key is to understand that if we laugh more often things could turn out differently.

Luey: Sam, you know the worst thing about growing old.
Sam: No... what's that?
Luey: What's What?

Newfound Funny

Share Your Life

When you have a few minutes, share your life. Be sure the subject matter is positive and uplifting—getting married, having a baby, or weekend adventures. Avoid talking about financial stresses, someone being sick, or someone dying, because that feeling you created will linger on after you leave.

Share your hobbies, pets, and children. People with dementia usually don't have the ability to go places and see people because it can be very stressful. Think about it—when is the last time they saw the moon and stars? Bring it to them in a story.

> *"I got to go the ocean last week. We walked out on this jetty, which is a man-made surface of huge stones going out about a mile into the ocean. The wind blew so hard you should have seen our wild hair when we got back to our cars. We couldn't even get our fingers through it. The waves were huge, and they crashed against the rocks with such force that if you were close to the edge you*

got soaked. The water tasted salty too. It was like eating salt straight out of the container. We went all the way to the end of this jetty and looked to the endless horizon of water. Ice blue water... just like in the movies. Every once in awhile you could see fishing boats and then they would be gone behind the enormous waves. Then we took our shoes off and walked along the beach. The water was so cold it numbed my feet, and it actually hurt. We picked up broken shells, I even saw a deep red colored starfish on one of the larger rocks. We ate at a nearby restaurant. They had the best clam chowder with these big onion rings. What else did we do?... Oh yea, we took a walk along the beach that night. When I closed my eyes, it was almost scary because the noise of the waves were so powerful I felt like it was going to crash on me. I must tell you it was an amazing experience. Have you been to the ocean before?"

When I had my first child, I was working in an Alzheimer's care center. A week after she was born, I brought her in and let the residents hold her. A staff member asked, "Aren't you afraid they might drop her?" I said reassuringly, "They know exactly what they are holding. It will be OK." Even a lady in the latest stage of Alzheimer's held her and perked up a bit making baby noises and clearly said "beautiful baby." That's a moment I will never forget. My mission is to tell others how we take too many things away from them to be on the safe side. We have literally taken away the most precious gifts we can give. If you still don't feel comfortable letting others hold your baby, just sit beside them with the baby in your arms. They love to just touch their little fingers. When my little girl got older, I brought her in and put her in the middle of the room and let her play for all to see. They gave me a gift with their *smiling faces. Even today my daughter enjoys going to care centers and singing for the people.*

If you play an instrument, crochet, tell a good story, or make great chocolate chip cookies—share these talents and irresistible things with people in facilities. Watching you do something you're good at may be a priceless gift to someone. We all have talents, and I know where you can find an appreciative audience.

Discover the magic within yourself!

Newfound Shared Treasure

enhanced moments

Drink Up

Whhat happens when a person is dehydrated? Health problems include: increased confusion, urinary tract infection, constipation, incontinence, decreased metabolism, headaches, daytime fatigue, intensified arthritis, pain, and decreased functioning. That's quite a list of symptoms, and both parties suffer the repercussions. So let's talk about ways to get someone to drink up!

Placing a pitcher of water beside their bed or a cup of water in front of them isn't enough. A person with dementia often loses his sense of thirst or is unable to tell you he is thirsty. Again, apply the concept that they only know what they see. You are more likely to create the thirst sensation by pouring ice-cold well water in front of him and adding verbal cues to stimulate his thirst. You might say, "I'm parched!" or "Let's wet our whistles" and even, "It's hot today."

The person may not be able to start a motion. If he has a blank look and doesn't pick up the glass, this is your cue to put your hand over his hand and kick start the motion.

Can they see the water in the glass? If you use Styrofoam cups, individuals probably cannot see anything in the cup. Try see-through colored glasses so the drink becomes Kool Aid to a person who doesn't like to drink water. You can also put the liquid in a McDonald's cup with a lid and straw and pretend they are drinking soda.

I was visiting a community and was in the mood to create a moment of joy by singing some wonderful old familiar tunes. While I was singing, I asked a staff person to get me a pitcher of water and a stack of cups. When the water arrived, I commented on how parched I was and offered drinks to the group. As I went around, of course, there were people who declined the drink of water. But a beautiful thing happened when I made a second pass. The people who declined the first time were now accepting the offer. I attributed that success to the fact that people with dementia only know what they see and their thirst sensation was stimulated by watching others drink up.

If someone is dehydrated or malnourished, he will function at a lower level. Possibly, he will display behaviors similar to those associated with Alzheimer's disease, but not actually have the disease at all.

A husband told me his solution concerning his wife who did not like to drink water but badly needed it. He knew what liquid his wife liked. So, he found a creative solution—he put water into shot glasses and they would do water shots together.

Serving warm liquids in the morning increases metabolism, and offering liquids after every activity is not only a way to take a break but also to hydrate. Of course, he wants coffee, coffee, and coffee…and 30 seconds after he drinks his coffee, he wants another cup. Use the short-term memory to your benefit and say over and over again. "The coffee is coming. I just started it." This gives a person hope that what they want will happen a little bit later. Caffeine dehydrates people, so you might want to serve decaffeinated coffee diluted with water.

Of course, you have to pick your battles. If he grows upset because you won't give him more coffee, and he refuses water or other liquids, by all means let him enjoy his coffee. The same could apply to a person who just wants to smoke a cigarette or to a diabetic person who wants something sweet.

The question becomes . . . Are three months of quality life better than three years of simply staying alive?

Newfound Desired Beverage

enhanced moments

Saturate
Their Obsessions

When a person has Alzheimer's they might start obsessing about a certain task or chore—washing their hair, hoarding dishes, peeling potatoes. If they are at the dinner table and constantly taking other peoples' cups or plates, just give them extra cups and plates when serving them. Saturate their obsessions.

Dowell was obsessed with shoelaces. He would take them out of other people's shoes and tie them in knots. First we tried taking away all the shoelaces and distracting him with activities or changing the subject. It didn't work. Then we gave him a box full of shoelaces and some shoes so he could do as he pleased. Not only was he busy for hours, but he was content.

Alice frequently commented how she would like to peel potatoes. At first everyone was concerned she would cut herself with the knife. When they found out peeling potatoes was a habit of a lifetime for Alice, they decided to bring her a five-gallon pail full of potatoes, and she peeled until she could peel no more.

Simplify. Simplify. Simplify. In the above story, you could boil potatoes and have her scrape the skin off with a table knife, although she might complain it isn't sharp enough or it isn't the right way to peel potatoes. Just bringing her the potatoes might be enough. Keep in mind that you need to know the person well and what their abilities are, but please give her a chance to fulfill her wishes.

Too often, we don't give people the chance to do what they want to do because we are concerned about their safety or we think they won't do it right. Don't play out in your mind what you think will happen. Try it! Then let go of your expectation for how it should be done.

Excerpt from "My Journey with Alzheimer's Disease"

I find that I am now a victim of obsessive behavior. Whatever I start, I want to get finished as soon as possible with no interruptions. An unfinished task preys on my mind until it is completely finished. This is the direct opposite of what I used to be. I was exhilarated by having dozens of balls bouncing in the air so that life did not become stale. Now I can only concentrate on one thing at a time, and, much to everyone's distress, this thing occupies my mind and obsesses me until it is completed.

When faced with a mountain, I will not quit!
I will keep on striving until I climb over,
find a pass through, tunnel underneath,
or simply stay and turn the mountaintop a gold mine—
with God's help!

Newfound Obsession and Solution

enhanced moments

Walking, Walking, Walking

Walking does wonders! It is a great way to hit all five senses and relieve stress for you and the person with dementia. It is also good exercise and helps us sleep better at night because of the vitamin D in the sun's rays. When you walk, notice the simple things in nature—the peace and quiet. Walk at least once a day and work up to twice a day. I cannot emphasize enough the positive benefits we all receive from walking. Even walking in the rain can be enjoyable for some.

> At three o'clock every day Lindel would become very upset and want to get out of the facility. If we ignored his anger, it would just get worse and start affecting the other residents. We needed a solution, so I started a routine. At 1:30 every afternoon I would take Lindel and a few other people that were good walkers on a stroll through the neighborhood. Sometimes, we would walk three times a day. The more we walked the better the day went. If we didn't go for walks, Lindel would become extremely

upset by 3:00 and want to go home. At this time, I would validate Lindel's feelings and say, "You know I need a break from this place, too. Can I join you?" He would rarely refuse because he knew he needed help finding his home. "Let me grab my coat and I will be right back." Then I would tell someone where I was going and to come look for us if we weren't back in an hour.

When we started our walk, I let him have an "illusion of control" by saying, "Which way should we go?" Lindel usually chose the same direction every time—away from traffic and toward residential homes. While walking the first block, I would let him blow off some steam and make small talk. At the corner, I still gave him "illusion of control" by saying again, "Now which way should we go?" I wouldn't hesitate with Lindel's decision and I showed him that I trusted him. Walking down the next block I would talk about his "treasures," which were fishing and his kids. "How many kids do you have?" "Boys or girls?" "Is it hard raising children?" "Can you give me any advice?" "Do you like to fish?" "You do? Well I have tried it a few times and only caught the small ones. How do you catch the big ones?"

When we came to the next corner I would say again, "Which way should we go?" and while Lindel was deciding I would innocently say, "I think this way looks good, what do you think?" (Illusion of choice) Because he didn't know which way to turn, he usually agreed with me. I started talking about different things like the nature around us, a pretty house, and the weather. The main purpose was to get his mind off his perceived problems and get him to like and trust me. When we got to the next corner and were heading toward the care center, I would say, "You know what, I think I recognize something down this street. Let's go this way." On good days, we walked right back to the facility. When he saw the facility he would say, "Hey, that looks familiar!" Then we walked back inside the building and he would say, "This is the exact floor plan of my house. Thank you for bringing me home. What's your name again? It was nice to meet you." In my heart I was saying, "Yea, you did it!" On other days it would take more than four blocks, sometimes we would walk over a mile. I could always get Lindel back to the facility eventually, but it wasn't always easy.

Although he was sometimes difficult to handle, Lindel was a blessing to others. Because of him, we started a walking program and everyone benefited from it. The walking program relieved stress and enabled some other residents to walk during the latest stages of the disease. Chair and bed alarms did not exist!

Few falls occurred, because in addition to walking, we had an exercise routine every morning, and a variety of physical activities throughout the day (sweeping the patio or clearing the tables). These physical activities help retain muscles, whereas restraints prevent a person from using her muscles. So, the activities complemented each another.

When we went for walks, if someone walked too far ahead I didn't say, "Therstin, come back!" (Now he thinks the CIA is after him.) I said, "Hey wait up for us!" In other words, mind your manners.

Letting a person walk out the door when they want can sometimes be a good thing. It not only gives an illusion of control but this may be the only way to help them realize that it is better inside the house. Use the plan of action in the previous story if they want to keep on walking.

I don't recommend that just anyone goes for these walks. It takes a person who is comfortable and confident with people who have Alzheimer's. And, it takes someone who remembers to put a few snacks in his pocket to share along the way.

I just want to share this thought that lies heavily on my heart. Perhaps it will help someone else. As John's pace slowed, (John had Alzheimer's) I didn't change mine. One day as we were walking up a small hill he asked, "Why do you always walk ahead of me?" Even today, the memory hurts. May we catch what we are doing before it becomes a sad memory.

–Joan

People with this disease think they are younger than they actually are and it makes them more mobile than most older people. When you hear about elderly ladies jumping over a fence without even tearing their skirts, now you'll know why—they are sixteen all over again!

I am going for a walk. Would you like to join me?

Newfound Walking Routine

Wandering

Wandering should not be labeled a bad thing. This person can still walk—that is a good thing. Is their wandering hurting anyone? No. Should we encourage people to walk? Yes. The more they are encouraged to walk the more they will retain muscles in their legs so they are less likely to fall. Will they fall? Yes. People will fall right next to you even when you are making every effort to prevent it. It is a risk, but life is full of risks, and the person should be allowed to take a risk if he chooses. That is dignity . . . honoring the person's wishes.

> My wife had about six months when she was very restless and would pace from one end to the other of our dead-end street for more than an hour. She didn't want me to walk with her, so I just let her go. I finally got smart and got a lawn chair, put it on the sidewalk, and sat down to watch her until she got tired. She no longer does this; some things get better.
>
> —Paul Edwards, husband and caregiver

They are giving you the opportunity to show them you respect their wishes, you respect their right to make decisions, and you love the essence of who they are. Be glad of the opportunity.

—Claudia Strauss

Newfound Wandering Path

Spread Holidays Throughout the Year

Holidays are usually very stressful for everyone, especially for a person with dementia. Not only do we take them out of their familiar environment but we also invite everyone over and ask them to be normal once again with the whole family.

Holidays usually bring the time when families first see something is wrong. Please change. Spread the holidays throughout the whole year. On Sunday, go to the Christmas church service. The next week invite one family for dinner. The next month, open presents one night and once or twice a month, schedule one family to visit and open presents. Keep events simple with a few people in a familiar environment and enjoy the simple blessings.

Excerpt from "My Journey into Alzheimer's Disease"

It is an old military maxim that the best generals win because they choose their battlefields carefully. The same thing is true with the early Alzheimer's patient. There are times when we cannot function and we need to withdraw and regroup. There are situations that we know we cannot handle. In spite of all the pushing and urging of friends and family who insist that we will have a wonderful time, the patient senses that it will lead to his mental devastation. There are times when the patient needs to be alone in order to keep everything in proper perspective, and the request to drop out of life or out of a situation at a particular time should be carefully considered.

At this point in my life, I can still sense when I need to retreat from some situations and my guess is that other patients have a better sense of what they should avoid than caregivers may be willing to give them credit for knowing.

If I do not listen to my body and withdraw from the overstimulation, it takes several days for my intellectual abilities to return. This is very frightening because I can't help wondering each time this happens if I've pushed myself totally over the line of no return.

When a person with Alzheimer's disease is still living at home, I encourage you to rethink the holiday tradition so it can be more enjoyable for the person with Alzheimer's, less stressful for the care provider, and easier for the family. Could it be that we inflict our values and standards on people with dementia?

Steps to help create happier, easier holidays

1.   Call a family meeting before the holidays. Discuss traditions that MUST be continued and traditions that are open to change.

2.   Make a MUST list and a SHOULD list. For example, I MUST buy gifts for my children. I SHOULD bake some holiday treats, but I COULD buy them at a local bakery. Try to do only those items on your MUST list.

3.   If large gatherings are uncomfortable for your loved one with Alzheimer's disease, but the family MUST all be together, set up a schedule for the day. Assign each family member an hour to be with your loved one, to take him outside for a walk if he is restless, to take her into the bedroom for much-needed quiet time. Make sure they are never left "alone in a crowd." The day will be much easier if someone is next to them saying things such as, "Here comes your son, Joe, and his daughter, Megan. Dinner is on the table. I will walk you to the dining room. Mom is taking the ham out of the oven. She will be here in just a minute."

4.   Ask for help. This sounds much easier than it is, especially if you are a person who is determined to do it all yourself. Try asking for small things at first. Maybe you MUST cook the turkey and the family's favorite stuffing, and you SHOULD make the trimmings, but you COULD ask each guest to help by bringing a vegetable.

5.   Put yourself first. Treat yourself during the holidays. Take your wife to an adult daycare an extra day each week. Take your neighbor up on the offer to take your husband out for drive. Take a nap. Read a good book. Exercise. Take deep breaths. Take a walk in the woods.

6.   It is important for family and friends to understand your situation and have realistic expectations. You might choose to write a letter:

> *Dear Family and Friends,*
> *As you are aware, Joe was diagnosed with Alzheimer's disease two years ago. We are looking forward to seeing you this holiday season, and we thought it might help for you to understand our situation before you arrive. I am enclosing a picture of Joe. As you can see he has changed*

quite a bit since you last saw him. Not only has he changed in looks, but some other things you might notice are _____(examples: does not know the people close to him, walks aimlessly in a circle through the living room, dining room and kitchen) I hope you understand that he may not recognize you. Please don't be offended. I hope you will treat Joe as you normally do. A smile and a hug mean so much. We cherish your friendship and are eager to see you.

Families need to work together to survive this disease. I've heard many stories how the oldest sibling is responsible for the parent. This journey cannot be done alone. Each sibling needs to play a role in taking care of a parent. Maybe the son handles the finances, the daughter sets up a schedule for when other relatives take care of the person.

The point is no one person can do this alone. By working together can we become strong. We need others. And we need a measure of peace.

If, as Herod, we fill our lives with the things, and again with things; if we consider ourselves so unimportant that we must fill every moment of our lives with action, when will we have the time to make the long, slow journey across the desert as did the Magi? Or sit and watch the stars as did the shepherds? Or brood over the coming of the child as did Mary? For each one of us, there is a desert to travel. A star to discover. And a being within ourselves to bring to life.

—Author Unknown

Newfound Tradition

Keys to Visiting

Understand that people with Alzheimer's may not recognize you. There's no need to put it to the test by saying this very common phrase, "My name is Helen. Do you remember me?" If you sense they are wondering who you are, simply introduce yourself by your first name like it is no big deal. So often, families and friends stop visiting because of an attitude of "what's-the-point when the person doesn't know who you are?" I assure you, they need your companionship and comfort now more than ever.

If they no longer recognize you try visiting as a friend instead of a daughter. When you begin the conversation by saying, "Hi Mom. It's me, Ruth," her wall goes up and she is less likely to talk because she is trying to figure out who this imposter is. In her mind, her kids are only kids, so you are too old to be her daughter. Instead try this:

"Hi. What a long day! Would you mind if I sat and relaxed for awhile?"

"Hi. It's so good to see you."

"You look comfortable. May I join you?"

"Hi. You're looking good today."

"Hello. I brought some ice cream I was hoping you would help me eat it."

"Hello. Do you like chocolate?" (Of course, you need to bring some chocolate with you.)

"Hi. I brought you something special."

When you visit it is a good idea to bring something with you to talk about and to move to a location that is quiet and away from high stimulation.

A daughter told me how much easier it was to visit with her mom if she brought her a gift. A small gift made them friends instantly. It worked like a charm, but it was getting expensive. So after awhile, she would sneak something from her mom's room before she left, take it home, and wrap it up again to give her the next time she visited. Sometimes she even would take home a pair of her mom's underwear, wash them, and bring them back the next day in a small gift box.

They are more likely to understand your words if you are looking at an item that reflects the conversation—old photos, a purse filled with stuff, a gift pertaining to their greatness like jewelry, fishing lures, Old Spice, perfume, a picture frame with familiar old photo, farmer's hat, favorite food, ice cream.

Excerpt from "Butterscotch Sundaes"

On Mother's Day, I took my mother something special from her past, her mother's purse. It was a small, beaded, cloth handbag filled with keepsakes that belonged to her mother (who died at a young age, but memories still lingered on in spite of my mom's Alzheimer's). When Mom opened the clasp of the handbag, she found several things inside that she could take out and hold in her hands—tiny gloves, fancy combs that were used in her mother's hair, a ring box with an opal ring, a small envelope and a note inside with her mother's handwriting, and a small portrait of her mother and father.

Very carefully, she took out everything; very carefully she put back everything. She smiled as she did it. She enjoyed smelling and touching everything. For a long time, Mom sat at the table and enjoyed the purse. She laid each thing on the table while we talked about her mother. Her favorite memory was seeing her mother brush her long brown hair as she stood in her bedroom in front of the mirror. She brushed it and then arranged it on the top of her head using the combs to keep it in place.

It is true that family heirlooms and keepsakes are irreplaceable. It is also true that you should not leave them with your loved one because they may get misplaced or hidden. But create a moment of joy by bringing them when you visit and then take them home again. Stuff isn't valuable until it brings a smile to someone's face.

While you are visiting, acknowledge other people who live there as if they are your friends. When they see you enjoying the company of others they are likely to join in and may even continue the camaraderie you created. Better yet, take a few minutes to share the fond memories and facts you know about your loved one with staff and other residents so they get to know the person not the disease.

If you're planning to go somewhere with your loved one, be sure to take 10 minutes to get reacquainted before you go. In her mind, you may be a "stranger" at first sight, even if you had a long visit yesterday.

Don't feel like you have to stay for a long period of time. The length of time is irrelevant but it is the quality of time that counts. (Where have you heard that one?)

Don't think you have to "talk" to create a moment. Just being there brings comfort. And practice, practice, practice. You will get better at visiting each time you go.

Another tidbit of advice—instead of complaining about what the staff is NOT doing, simply see this as an opportunity for you to give back the many gestures of love your mother or father so generously gave to you as a child.

I received an e-mail from a daughter who was very frustrated during her visits with her mom because she could not understand why her mother did not care about her appearance. Her hair was a mess, she didn't put on makeup anymore, she was untidy and she would simply sit and rock in her chair all day long. It was not like her mom. I wrote back and made some suggestions for her next visit and here is how she replied.

"I took your advice and massaged my mom's hands and arms with lotion, I combed her hair, applied a little makeup, and put on one of her necklaces (which she wanted to pay me for). Then she asked where we were going. I took her for a short walk and she was just

beaming. I have not seen her that happy in a long time. You are right! It was my attitude which determined how our visit would go. Thank you for letting me know it's the simple things you do that mean the most and to accept my mom as she is. I cannot change her but I can enjoy her. I can remember the good times with her and smile at the smiles she gives me now.

In the middle to late stages of Alzheimer's, it is sometimes difficult to know how the person wants to be taken care of because they have lost the ability to communicate. The question to ask is, "How did your spouse take care of you when you weren't feeling so well? How did your mom take care of you? What did your dad do to show you he loved you?" Here are some of the answers I have received.

A hug, rubbed my back, cuddled me with a warm blanket, gave me chicken soup, 7-UP, Vicks VapoRub, warm tapioca pudding, cold hand on my forehead, warm wash cloth, stroked my hair, hot tea, jabbed me on the shoulder, went for a walk, made warm bread with butter after school, sat with me etc., etc. Notice how all of these things are very simple.

List the ways they showed you love, then next time you visit do one of those things. If they loved you that way, that is probably the way their mom showed them love. Share what you found with staff and other family so we can all show them love the way they need to be loved until the end. That kiss on the forehead may be their mountaintop.

I've learned that even when I have pains, I don't have to be one.

Newfound Ways to Say Hello

Windows In The Brain
by Fay Risner

*W*hen we are born, our brain is full of well-lit, airy, vacant rooms with an open window in each one. Knowledge and experiences flow through the open window to fill the rooms as we grow, and flow back out as we mentally call on them to create the type of human being we become. Imagine if by the time you are in your sixties, you were to find yourself searching for a thought in the memory room. You find that the room had become dark, the drapes drawn. You strain to see the familiar object you are searching for in your mind, trying to remember what it looked like the last time you saw it, but you can't find the object in the dark.

That's what happens to a person who is afflicted with Alzheimer's disease. One such person was a large-framed, boisterous farmer who spoke with a salty vocabulary. First, the memory room in his brain became dark, then other rooms darkened as they were covered with a black shroud called plaque that continued slowly to spread from room to room. As it entered the open windows, the plaque closed them, and the drapes drew shut to put out the light. As this happened to the farmer, he became a shell of the man his family and friends once knew and was admitted to a care center. In time, he forgot how to feed himself, had trouble with swallowing, couldn't do his activities of daily living skills, and could barely stand long enough to transfer from the bed to the wheelchair. The only vocabulary he had left was loud profanity unless he chose to parrot short sentences he heard from the aides such as "It's time to eat." Or "It's bedtime."

There came a time when the farmer quit repeating what he heard. His face became expressionless, and his eyes stared vacantly. I was sure that most of the windows in his brain had shut, become locked, and would never reopen again. I was wrong!

Since the farmer was in his room most of the day, I had taken to seating him in the living room with the other residents after the evening meal. I hoped people talking and Vanna White flashing across the television would stimulate his mind. As time went by, I gave up hope that what I was doing would trigger anything in the farmer that I would see outwardly, but I consoled myself with the idea that I didn't know what was happening inside those dark rooms in his brain. You know how the window frame in an old house doesn't fit quite tight, and a small amount of air seeps between the sill and the frame? I thought maybe that might be how the windows in the farmers' mind were working, so I felt I shouldn't give up trying to stimulate him even if I couldn't see I was helping him.

One evening at bedtime, I was pushing the farmer's wheelchair across the living room. As we neared a visitor, sitting by his wife, the visitor reached out his hand and patted the farmer's knee.

"Hello" the visitor greeted.

"Hello" the farmer returned in this booming voice and he called the man by name. The blank expression on the farmer's face had changed to one of joy at seeing an old friend.

"He knows you!" I exclaimed in surprise as I realized the farmer recognized the visitor, and he actually spoke with out repeating another person's sentence. The farmer's eyes remained focused on the visitor.

"He should," the visitor replied. "We've been friends for years, and we were both on the board of business in town for along time, weren't we?"

"Yes," the farmer answered with gusto.

I could see a calm look of contentment on this face as the memory room's window crept open to let the memories I had been so sure were trapped forever in darkness.

"We went to a lot of those board meetings together," the visitor continued. He patted the farmer's knee again as he said, "This is the man who made a lot of the important decisions at the meetings, didn't you?"

Tears welled up in the farmer's eyes as he struggled to grasp memories long forgotten. I hated to see him so sad, and I didn't want this to be an uncomfortable situation for him or the visitor so I tried to add a little humor to the conversation.

"Oh sure! Were those important decisions what time to go get the beer after the meetings were over?"

Both men laughed at my teasing as the farmer slowly boomed out, "Yes!"

I explained to the visitor that it was the farmer's bedtime so he had to leave. By the time I had wheeled the farmer the short distance down the hall, into his room and closed the door, the farmer's face was expressionless again. His eyes stared vacantly, focused on the drapes behind the bed which were closed across the window just like the pair that darkened the window shut again in his mind.

enhanced moments

Newfound Ways to Open Windows to the Brain

"Who Are You?"

When he thinks you are his wife but you are his daughter. When she thinks you are her mom but you are her sister. When she thinks you are her daughter but you are her granddaughter. When he thinks you are a stranger but you are his friend. Be whomever they want you to be . . . you are more likely to create a moment if you simply "go with it."

A daughter shared how when her father would become upset she would become his secretary. He was a businessman and always had a secretary. She would get her pad and pencil and sit down in front of him and at first ask very simple questions that only needed yes and no answers. As they continued, she noticed how his words became sentences and sentences became paragraphs. She was amazed how his communication improved. Becoming his secretary for the moment gave him a sense of comfort, security, and importance.

Grown children of Alzheimer's parents often express their frustration and emotional pain to me of how their mom or dad no longer recognizes them. They understand that their loved one has a disease. But they are baffled that their dad can recognize his wife, but doesn't recognize him as his son. I believe they remember their spouse, because the spouse was always an adult in their memories. But their children they remember as children.

> *I walked into a memory care community and a gentleman came up and gave me the biggest hug and told me it had been so long since he had seen me. I replied, "Yes, it has. It is so good to see you."*
>
> *Soon after a caregiver came up and said, "Bob, this lady is just visiting. It's not . . . " I wanted to say, "Stop it!!" I could have been his long-lost friend. I could have been his neighbor. I could have been his sister. I could have been an old girlfriend. I could have been someone familiar who he would have chatted with like old times.*

If someone doesn't cooperate with you or has great anger toward you, but you have done nothing to create that anger, consider the possibility that you look like someone they have never liked. Don't take it personally. Simply request that someone else be their caregiver.

> *There is a gentleman who loves to dance. I call him "Pa," and he calls me "Ma." I tell him, "It's Friday night, and we're going dancing. First we'll stop at Red's (bar that used to be in town), and we'll have a couple of drinks. Then we'll go dancing." It brings a smile to his face every time. The next day, I ask him if he's tired, because we danced all night. He smiles from ear to ear.*
>
> —Luonne Whitford

Blessed is that person who comes up to me and tells me his name first and reminds me of some experience we have shared. Usually this kind of approach on their part suddenly triggers a flow of memories that is almost impossible for me to recall by just reaching into the blankness.

—Robert Davis

Newfound Response to "Who are you?"

enhanced moments

Show of Affection

When you were younger and you visited your grandma, what was her way of showing you her love? Did she hug you? Did she have a special name for you? Did she sit and rock you? Did she make you cookies? Did she gently do your hair? I believe the answer you discover provides the very way for you to show them in some way your love for them.

A young lady told me how when she visited her grandma she would run inside the house and her grandma would reach down her hand to her cheek and say endearingly, "Oh sweet girl." Now that her grandma is older and almost always in bed, when she visits she reaches over to her grandma's cheek and says, "Oh sweet girl." My grandma has not forgotten this gesture of love.

The following story is from a Christmas letter sent to me from Ora Mae, whose sister has Alzheimer's, and is a wonderful example of "Show of Affection."

Christmas finds Lahoma and I, ages 83 and 82, sharing a love that has been strong since my earliest remembrance.

At ages 6 and 5, we walked a path through the hilly fields carrying our books and lunch in a little basket. It was Lahoma that carried the basket, helped me over the "sty" in the fence, eased my fears of the big bull in an adjacent field, and protected me from the teasing of eighth-grade boys and girls. And so it continued through elementary school and high school. Life was lonely and fearful when the sister whose arm I went to sleep on every night, left for college.

Our friend recently sent us the book, "ALWAYS SISTERS," by Christine Rossetti:

> *"For there is no friend like a sister,*
> *In calm or stormy weather*
> *To cheer one on the tedious way;*
> *To fetch one if one goes astray,*
> *To lift one if one totters down,*
> *To strengthen...by standing by."*

Alzheimer's disease has caused my heroine to "totter" down. Her fantasies are daily concerning helping where there are needs. Many "small children" are with us day and night to be cared for. What do Lahoma and I share? Not much concerning daily events or problems, which she can't understand, but the great love in abundance expressed by gracious words of love, hugs and kisses and closeness.

My Christmas message to you, my family and friends, is that to be the one who "stands and strengthens" as she "totters down" is my life and joy!

I'll close with a prayer I heard her praying softly as I tucked her in the other night:

"Jesus, thank you for Mae. She is so good to me. She loves me and she loves you so much. Help her to sleep tonight. She will have to get up early to go to school tomorrow. Thank you, Jesus. Amen."

Remember—Love does it!

Yours in Love,
Ora Mae

Newfound Show of Affection

enhanced moments

"Honey" "Dearie" "Sweetie"

A frequent question asked is "Is it OK to call them Honey or Sweetie?" I believe if they are addressing you as "Honey" or "Sweetie" then that is your cue to address them in the same manner.

If they were a businessman or school teacher, they may want to be addressed as Mr. Evans, professor, boss or Mrs. Larsen, and would be offended if you called them "Honey." A man of the greatest generation is not "cute." He is handsome or charming.

It is worth the time to figure out what their friends called them. In their care plan their name may be Frances Guthrey. But you can clearly see he doesn't respond to Frances because his friends called him Buz.

A lady in the audience at one of my Enhanced Moments seminars explained that she would recognize the name "Dutch" even though many knew her as "Laurie." As a child she would talk and talk and talk and no one understood what she was saying so they said she was talking in "Dutch." And the name has stuck even though she is now in her 40s.

Some people feel it isn't age appropriate to use "Honey," "Dearie," or "Sweetie." I would agree that is true in some situations, especially if they do not consider who this person is. But it is also true that another person might prefer to be called "Grannie" or "Dearie" or "Dutch."

> *During a training session staff explained to me that they were given instructions not to call this lady "Grannie" because it was demeaning. By the end of the discussion, clearly the majority would testify that this particular lady lit up when she was addressed as "Grannie" and befriended and cooperated with caregivers who called her "Grannie." So, how can "Grannie" be wrong?*

Too often we think what is right and wrong is black and white. With Alzheimer's, nothing is black or white. We are all different. When you meet one person with Alzheimer's, you have simply met one person. Everyone who has this disease is different.

So, when you are in the process of deciding what you should and should not do, the individual person and the individual situation should be your guide. Your guide should NOT be… "Well that didn't work for this other person, so I don't think it will work for her." Instead, you should gather as much information about each person and make your decision from that information. It is also NOT about what you would want. It's about what *this* person would want.

They say no two snowflakes are alike, well no two cases of dementia are alike either. This disease affects everyone differently. Including families.

—Sally Dutra

Newfound Term of Endearment

Outings with Less Stress

Before you leave a care center with your loved one, sit and visit for about 10 minutes to get reacquainted. Because of her short-term memory loss, you will seem like a stranger and she may be nervous about leaving with you—even if you had a nice, long visit the day before.

Simplify outings by going on short country drives, visiting a friend at her house, watching children play at a park, feeding ducks, or going for a walk in a quiet neighborhood. Avoid eating out at restaurants especially during prime hours. If you really want to go out to eat, ask for a private room away from the noise and rush. Avoid malls and zoos; these places just aren't familiar and have too much stimulation.

On the other hand, if the person is enjoying herself at a mall, then you know it is OK. Use the rule of thumb again....If it works, it works! If it doesn't, it doesn't! To figure our whether it worked or not, be aware of the person's emotions. If she seems really confused or anxious, you know you will have to change and try something else or simplify your outing. If the person lives in a care center, call and ask the staff how the person is doing when you get home.

Try anything once and don't assume he won't like it. This way you won't miss out on a possible moment of joy.

Gladys had to leave her farmhouse and move into a near-by care center. She had always been a very proper, well-mannered lady. The family decided to take her out for a drive. When they brought her back, she would not go inside. She wanted to go home. The staff insisted this was her home, and she needed to get inside. After a while they resorted to forcing her back into the facility but that didn't work either. Even though she was a little lady with gray hair, weighing only 100 pounds, she won that battle. A third person came along and observed the situation and nonchalantly walked up to the lady and said, "Gladys, your daughters are inside waiting to eat lunch with you. Are you hungry?" She said yes and walked inside the building. It was that easy. Unfortunately, the family is scared to take their mother on an outing again because of this incident. This happens all too often, and we keep taking things away because we are scared of what might happen. Soon the person with dementia ends up with very little in their lives. In this situation, we should treasure the solution that was found and use it over and over again.

A group of people just got back from a bus trip and one gentleman wouldn't get off the bus. Many people tried to coax him off the bus but after an hour he still sat. A staff person remembered that he didn't like loud music. They

turned up the radio, and he immediately got off the bus.
Creative solutions work! Think outside the box!

Celebrate the Seasons!

If the person is unable to go on outings, celebrate the seasons inside. For example, in the spring bring in baby animals, plant a flowering bush outside their window, talk about the farmers in the fields or bring in a pot of tulips so they can enjoy the miracle of growth. In the summer, bring them fresh strawberries, open a window to give the free gift of fresh warm air, sit in the backyard, soak their feet in a wading pool while drinking a glass of fresh lemonade, or stop and smell the roses, better yet, the lilac bushes. In the fall, share the harvest, the turning leaves, or take a nature walk. In the winter, break off icicles just like you did when you were little and share with others. Together talk about the feeling of the cold wet icicle melting in your mouth and slipping through your fingers. Stop and see the miracles in the simple things of daily living. I'd bet you will receive as many gifts of joy as you give away.

Excerpt from "My Journey with Alzheimer's Disease"

Leaving the routine of being around my familiar home, having more people and excitement around than I am accustomed to, varying my ritual for taking care of my grooming and health care, being able to lie down and nap at my usual time, all brought me to a place of being unable to make even the most basic decisions for myself, of not being aware of how to relieve my discomfort. This experience taught me that if I want to function at the top of my limited capacity, I must establish a routine and keep to it. I must stay away from crowds, blinking lights, too much emotional or mental stimulation, and must not become physically exhausted. I have to set the bounds of my playpen, even though it is annoying to give up the freedom of "hanging loose." I must seek out social contacts in groups of ten or less. I must avoid shopping centers and large athletic stadiums.

However, I can still work in the yard, I can enjoy church services and my friends there, and I can still go out in the midst of nature. The most important thing is finding out where I become the most lost and confused, and then staying away from those places so that I can enjoy life in my safe "playpen." Right now, I am very happy in my playpen, yet I realize that it will grow smaller and I will be compelled to adjust to this if I am to function at my highest level.

Right now, I am just sitting here being thankful that wrinkles don't hurt.

Newfound Outing

Saying Goodbye

Saying goodbye is never easy, but hopefully I can make it easier. When you are getting close to departing start to make comments that leave them with positive "feelings." Feelings of assurance. Feelings of self worth. Feelings of being loved. Feelings they have loved you. Feelings that everything is OK "for the moment."

"Let's pray before I go."
"I wish I was as feisty as you."
"I wish I was smart as you."
"I thank you for your advice."
"Can I visit you again?"
"I really enjoyed talking with you."
"You always look out for me."
"I'm glad we got to talk."
"I enjoyed your company so much."
"This has been lovely."
"I haven't laughed so hard in a long time. Thank you."
"Your smile always makes my day."

Leaving them with a feeling that they have helped you in some way can create amazing responses. People need to be needed no matter what the age or their physical/mental ability. If the person were a teacher, ask her to edit a paper or help a younger person with their homework. If they were a mechanic, describe the noise coming from your car and give them the opportunity to tell you what they think it is. If they had children, ask for advice on discipline. If they were a doctor/nurse, describe some symptoms and get their diagnosis.

People need to feel needed. And, who knows, the advice they give you will probably work.

Excerpt from "Living in the Labyrinth"

If I am no longer a woman, why do I still feel I'm one? If no longer worth holding, why do I crave it? If no longer sensual, why do I still enjoy the soft texture of satin and silk against my skin? If no longer sensitive, why do moving song lyrics strike a responsive chord in me? My every molecule seems to scream out that I do, indeed, exist, and that existence must be valued by someone!

If you need to leave for a short time to talk with someone privately, give the person a reason for your departure that they would understand.

"I need to use the bathroom.
"I'm going to get a drink."
"I need to get _____. I'll be right back."

These excuses work if you add a matter-of-fact tone of voice. If you need to leave for awhile, give them the hope you will be back soon and give them a place where they couldn't go with you. "I need to go to work, but I'll see you soon." Or, identify a place they wouldn't want to go: "I have to go to the dentist to get my tooth pulled." Avoid saying "I have to go home now." Because that will trigger them to want to go home, too. Instead say, "I'll see you again soon!"

Caregivers frequently feel like they can't leave the person with dementia. However, with short-term memory loss you can leave because when you get back, they will forget that you were gone!

When leaving, it helps to give hugs, a reassuring touch, a smile or familiar words that say you care. The bottom line is if you are comfortable with saying goodbye, she will be more comfortable with your departure.

> *People will forget what you said,*
> *People will forget what you did,*
> *but they will never forget*
> *how you made them feel .*

Newfound Ways to Say Goodbye

enhanced moments

Face the Challenges

There are a variety of challenges you will have to face head on. I encourage you to take everyday situations more lightly and choose your battles.

Loss of Emotional Control

In the beginning stages the negative emotional outbursts are created by fear. They realize at this point something is wrong and fear creates anger, frustration, tears, depression, suspiciousness, etc. The beginning stages of Alzheimer's are the most difficult. Trust me when I say it usually gets better when they regress to the middle stages of Alzheimer's. During the middle stages they don't remember that they don't remember.

> *I am glad she can forget she has Alzheimer's disease and that she doesn't have to hold that worry up to herself continually as if it were a mirror in which she was always seeing herself.*
>
> —David Dodson Gray

When someone is upset about something repeat these magical words "I am sorry. I am sorry. I did not mean to hurt you. I am sorry it is my fault. I am sorry, that should not have happened." The person is less likely to hold onto the anger if your tone of voice is truly sorry. Even if you didn't do anything wrong simply say, "I am sorry." It is truly magical.

Another suggestion when they are angry is to leave the room and come back with another approach five minutes later (with cookies in hand). If they ask you to leave them alone, then leave them alone! If you are giving them care and they resist, know that it is only going to get worse if you insist. Again, simply leave and come back with another approach.

If you witness an angry gentleman or two men arguing, confidently walk up to them, extend your hand for a handshake, and in a deep, strong voice introduce yourself and ask if there is anything you can do to help. A handshake is a friendly gesture that triggers men to be gentlemen.

It is easier to keep someone happy and content first, than trying to calm someone down after he becomes upset.

Hitting

When a person is agitated or frustrated, our instinct is to redirect them. This could cause more agitation and frustration. To diffuse the angry person, whistle happily before you enter the person's room. Or you might say, "You seem upset. Did someone make you mad?" And then listen. "That shouldn't have happened. I will check on it for you." Force yourself to let go of the fear of being hit, and know that being near them may be the best way to bring comfort.

On a scenic drive one afternoon, a man in the car kept telling me he was going to charge me with kidnapping. When it was time to unload the van, I was sure I was going to get hit. I asked him about his stress. I reaffirmed his frustrations, and said that it was his Alzheimer's Disease that made it difficult to understand. He visibly calmed down—and inquired about why he was so stupid. I reminded him that he was not stupid, but he just had Alzheimer's, which messes with his mind. Not only was he not stupid, I told him, I could tell from some previous conversations that he is very intelligent. I told him that together we will find ways to outsmart his brain. He agreed to the challenge.

—Sheila, a friend of mine who is an inspiration

I believe hitting is directly related to us not understanding their needs and adding too much stress to their lives. Sometimes the only way for them to communicate is to hit. Hitting is a way to say, "Stop, I can't handle this!" or "Back off!" You need to respect their wishes. Much of what they do is a reaction from outside stimulation.

A caregiver was trying to get a woman to give a urine sample and got hit. I stepped in and asked the person to sit down and have a cup of coffee with me, because she seemed stressed. She admitted to being stressed and sat down. I asked her why she was stressed, and she told me. By listening closely, I sifted through the garbled sentences and learned that she was worried about something in her basement. I said I was having the same problem in my basement and when her husband solves their problem, I could use his advice to fix mine. I then said I had to go to the bathroom, and asked if she did, too. She did and the caregiver got her urine sample.

—Sheila

Another approach is called the "Good Guy, Bad Guy." When a caregiver is struggling, another caregiver should step in and rescue the person. (She is the "Good Guy.") She should boldly say, "Get out of here! You are not being nice." This makes the person feel like someone is sticking up for them. And the person with dementia is more likely to cooperate with someone who sticks up for them.

Losing Items

When they forget where they put things, they automatically think someone must have taken the items, so their next thought is that they need to hide their things. Because of short-term memory loss, they forget where they hid the items. It becomes a vicious, never-ending cycle. One health care provider told about some of the strange places she found things: an iron in the oven, ice cream in the linen closet, watch in the sugar bowl, milk in the freezer, jewelry in the microwave, and underwear in a purse. Some of these hiding places make sense if you think about where they are living in their mind. Accept the fact that many things will get misplaced.

> *In a facility, they started losing very expensive items like glasses, dentures, and hearing aids. Families became very upset, and staff spent countless hours trying to find these items. One day they walked unexpectedly into a gentleman's room while he was trying to hide these items. Guess where his hiding place was. You couldn't begin to guess. He hid these items in the ceiling. Yes, he figured out that the tiles in the ceiling could be moved. He stepped on a chair and tucked them neatly out of sight.*

My recommendation to you is to stop trying to find things. Items that are lost usually show up sooner or later. In this case, the staff could have looked forever, wasting valuable time that could have been spent sitting down and talking with someone. Get a marker board and write "LOST" at the top of it. When families or anyone is trying to find something, write it down.

It is important that they get their eyes checked while they can still successfully complete an eye exam. As the disease progresses, they may lose the ability to take an eye exam. Keep that prescription on file so if they do lose their glasses (which will probably happen) you can easily order a new pair of glasses without going through unnecessary frustration.

There are some things you learn best in calm, and some in storm.

—Willa Cather

Newfound Challenge

enhanced moments

Intimacy

Intimacy , or sexuality, often gets ignored. However, intimacy and sexual activity are a very normal part of adult life. Control of sexuality is thought to be located in the limbic system which is damaged from Alzheimer's disease. So the person may be sexually active or may lose interest in sex. Intimacy should not be confused with sex. Many times a person simply craves the touch of another person. Those who need touch the most, receive touch less often. Staff must be trained to touch appropriately and frequently, including holding hands or simply touching their face or patting their backs.

Questions that may help understand life habits

Do they have an affectionate family?
Has the person ever slept in bed alone?
What is the person's sexual orientation?
Was there any history of sexual abuse?

At-home caregivers may struggle with the changing needs of a person with Alzheimer's disease. The spouse may choose to sleep in a separate bed or bedroom so they can get enough sleep. Mary, a wife in her early 60s who is caring for her husband, told this story:

> *George and I had a wonderful day. He was more alert than normal. We visited our daughter and had a picnic by the lake. On the ride home, George was able to respond to my comments and seemed very happy and relaxed. Once home, we went into the bedroom to get ready for bed. As I started to undress, George started crying and pushing me out the door. After calming him down, it became apparent that he was confused—he believed I was our daughter. The fact that he thought our daughter was undressing in front of him and that he didn't recognize me as his wife were the most devastating things that have happened so far in this disease. I had hoped that this may be a night when I could once again sleep in his arms. I ended up in the guest room, alone.*

Mary is rightfully grieving for the husband she is losing.

> *Bob, who has Alzheimer's, and Betty, his wife, went to a restaurant with several other family members one evening. Bob and Betty were seated next to each other. Suddenly Bob felt lost and could not see Betty. Betty simply turned to him and said, "I am right here, Bob. I'm Betty, your wife." Bob, with much love and adoration in his eyes, touched Betty's face lightly and commented, "And you're so beautiful." What a blessing for Betty to know that Bob thought she was beautiful after 59 years of marriage.*

Be sure both parties are capable of consensual sex. Every situation is different and know that you are not alone. Sharing your story in a support group and with others will help. No one can get through these losses alone.

I will never forget when a wife said to me about her husband who lived in a care center, "I know I cannot be with my husband 24 hours a day so I'm glad someone loves him when I cannot."

It's important to know that sometimes, when a spouse is affectionate toward another resident, the other resident often resembles his wife. So in his mind, he is loving his wife.

The sexual part of the marriage may be over, however, with education and support, the long- shared intimacy between two people may be sustained. Sex is less about the act and more about the need to feel loved.

The best and most beautiful things in the world cannot be seen or touched but are felt in the heart.
—Helen Keller

Newfound Love

enhanced moments

Moments
of Discomfort

Moments of Discomfort was written by Lori Linton Nelson. She is working on a grant through the Hartford Institute on Geriatric Nursing at New York University to improve pain management delivery in the elderly population. On a personal note, she is a friend who has her heart in this profession and possesses a wealth of knowledge.

Pain can often be a culprit for behavioral symptoms such as generalized irritability, pacing, increased wandering, anxiety, resistance to care activities, and depression-like symptoms. The person suffering from dementia may not be able to verbally communicate that they are feeling pain. It may be difficult for them to differentiate pain from another health problem. They do know, however, that they are feeling discomfort.

As caregivers, we must often make assumptions about the individual with dementia. We do this by basing observational information about the person and comparing it to other experiences we have had.

This is an important tool but cannot be the only tool. Pain can be assessed by using simple questioning and screening tools. Many people can use a pain intensity scale, such as 1 to 10.

Caregivers may want to try out several versions. Some caregivers find it helpful to use an intensity scale with faces, similar to what children are offered in hospitals. Sometimes we need to find the right words (those that make sense to the individual with dementia) to use in order to describe their pain. Asking them whether they "hurt" or "feel badly" in an area of their body may be helpful, or talking with family members and asking how they have historically acted when in pain.

In addition, it is helpful to review their medical history to determine whether there are current or past medical problems that cause them to be in pain now. Arthritis, osteoporosis, chronic back pain, gout, stroke, history of multiple fractures, or diabetes are examples of conditions which can cause both acute and chronic pain. These need to be reviewed with the individual's health care provider, so that the appropriate interventions are pursued.

At times, it is so difficult to differentiate pain from other sources of frustration, that a caregiver may need to discuss a trial of regularly scheduled pain medication with the health care provider. Monitoring the use of regularly scheduled pain medication and assessing a decrease in suspected pain-related behaviors is helpful in determining whether pain is present and then relieved, or whether the agitation is from a different source.

Most individuals with dementia also respond to non-medication type remedies. These include: hot and cold treatments, relaxation, distraction, and massage. These remedies should be considered, along with pain medication, by the individual's health care provider.

Margaret's favorite song to sing over and over again was, "Sing a song of sixpence." She had nine children and her joy was to nip off the person's nose who was sitting next to her. Four years passed and I went to visit Margaret. I found her lying on her bed in a fetal position and moaning in slight pain. I laid down next to her and softly sang, "Sing a song of sixpence, a pocket full of rye. Four and twenty black birds..." She whispered, "baked in a pie." I continued, "When the pie was opened, the birds..." She whispered, "began to sing." I continued, "Wasn't that a dainty dish to set before the King." And in the end I nipped off her nose. My wish was that everyone would have known her favorite song and they sang it whenever they had the chance. I believe her pain might have been a little less.

There was a gentleman who earned a reputation as an escape artist. One day, he started to hit the aides who were trying to stop him from leaving the building. I took him for a walk outside. After a couple of minutes he started to limp. He told me he was supposed to get his toes amputated. I didn't know if he was confused or if he truly had pain in his feet. On our way back, I asked him to hold the door open for me to get back into the building and luckily it worked. Once inside, he was no longer hitting and kicking. He asked the aides to take care of me while he took care of business. Later I found out that two toes were quite swollen from ingrown toenails. The next day his son took him to the doctor to get his feet taken care of. He continued to be an escape artist but I believe the hitting was caused from his pain.

—Sheila, a very insightful person

*If their behavior is different today than yesterday,
it is probably not the disease, but pain!*

—Jolene

Newfound Discomfort

Letting Go
of Expectations

In the middle stages of Alzheimer's, their developmental level is eight years old. As the disease progresses, their development level is five or younger. In the late stages of Alzheimer's, their developmental level is three or younger. If you have grandchildren or children three or younger, watch what they are able to do and a person with Alzheimer's can probably do it, too. As the disease progresses their development regresses in almost the same way as an infant grows.

The same pattern applies for inhibitions. While a child has not yet formed inhibitions, the adult with dementia loses his inhibitions. For example, when a child has a thought, does he stop and think, "I shouldn't say that." No, children say exactly what they are thinking.

The same is true for people with dementia. I believe that is why swearing is so prevalent. It is not that they don't understand those words; it is just that they have lost the ability to filter their thoughts before they speak.

What's one of the first words a child says? No. What is one of the last words a person with dementia can say? No. And, just like a toddler, communication can be expressed with body language and outward emotions (cries, tantrums, hitting) instead of verbal communication. When someone is unable to communicate with words, the next defense is physical.

Now think about clothing and how that corresponds to a child's developmental stage. At what age does your child want to wear the same outfit everyday? I have three children and I know the age is four to six. At what age does your child wear clothes inside out, underwear on the outside, purple with green, layers and layers of clothes, and think they are cute just because they dressed themselves? Around three. At what age does your child love to be naked? Three and younger. This is the same progression for someone with Alzheimer's. They lose their inhibitions as the disease progresses, just as a child gains his inhibitions as he matures.

When my son was 1 and playing in the sand pile, he would shovel sand into his mouth like it was candy. I thought of Dowell, another person who taught me many lessons. In the late stages of his dementia, Dowell would eat flowers and dirt. Instead of correcting him, I wish I could have understood that this was his developmental level and I should have replaced the dirt with a graham cracker.

When my daughter was 3, she asked if she could help me clear the tables. I was thinking, "No Way!" She might break my dishes. She wouldn't know where to put them. But then a light bulb went on! She could sort my silverware. Then I thought, people with dementia could sort silverware, too. Sure enough, another purposeful activity had been created.

In the late stages of dementia, some people put everything in their mouths. If you put lotion in a lady's hands, she might try to lick it off her hands. Too often, we make the conclusion this person cannot have lotion anymore. I disagree. We should still give her lotion but we need to take the next step and rub it in for her. With this awareness of the challenges that occur in each developmental level, I celebrate because it helps me understand a person with Alzheimer's.

There is definitely a difference, though, in the language and tone of voice (high pitch) we use for babies compared to the language and tone of voice (low pitch) we use for older people. This also does not mean we treat older people like children. This means we understand and accept the capabilities of a person with Alzheimer's.

A person with dementia needs structure and routine, as children do. What if you took your child to preschool and they didn't have any structure? Basically they could run around and do what they wanted to all day. What would their emotions be like when you picked them up? Some kids would be crying, some kids would be fighting, some kids would be scared, some kids would be clinging to the adults, some kids probably would wander off or other kids would say, "I want to go home." Memory care communities need to have a structured program every day.

"Let Go"

To "let go" does not mean to stop caring;
it means I can't do it for someone else.

To "let go" is not to cut myself off;
it's the realization that I can't control another.

To "let go" is to admit powerlessness,
which means the outcome is not in my hands.

To "let go" is not to try to change or blame another;
it's to make the most of myself.

To "let go" is not to "care for," but to "care about."

To "let go" is not to judge,
but to allow another to be a human being.

To "let go" is not to deny, but to accept.

To "let go" is not to nag, scold, or argue, but instead to
search out my own shortcomings and correct them.

To "let go" is not to regret the past, but to grow and live
for the future.

To "let go" is to fear less and love more.

Newfound Way to Let Go

Good Dementia,
Bad Dementia

There are good memories and there are bad memories. It is important for anyone who is giving care to be informed of both. Maybe she witnessed a murder. Maybe he served in the war. Maybe she was molested. Maybe he had a tragic accident at an early age. Maybe she is a survivor of the Holocaust. The bad memories are still very vivid in a person's mind even if they haven't told anyone.

It can be described as a ridge on their brain and the person goes over that ridge frequently. With dementia it may even feel like they are truly living the memory over again, as if it is actually happening that moment.

Angela would have screaming episodes and we would try to console her and find out why she was crying. We later found out she had been molested when she was a child. Knowing this gave us the words and actions she needed. When she would scream we would say, "I'm not going to let anyone hurt you. I am here Angela." We also knew that some male caregivers would not be able to care for her because of the memories it might trigger. But had we not found out this bad memory, I believe her screaming would have been labeled as part of the disease process.

Strong, vivid, tragic, painful memories are not forgotten even in dementia.

A nurse was doing a physical evaluation on a lady in the late stages of dementia. This lady was non-responsive and bedridden. When she began to check the lady's head she felt a huge ridge across her skull. The nurse was startled and said aloud, "What happened there?" The lady piped up clear as day, "Do you want to hear about that? When I was a child I fell off a stone wall and it cracked my skull. People pampered me because of that." And then she was gone again. The clarity of the lady's words astonished the nurse, but can you imagine how many times she must have told her story? It was certainly not forgotten.

A wife shared her story about her husband who had Alzheimer's. When he was nine, he asked his mom for a baby brother. Unfortunately, his mom died while giving birth to his baby brother. Still to this day, he blames himself for the death of his mom. Because of his dementia, his feelings are as strong now as they were when he was a child.

For those of you who don't have dementia, I would like for you to consider something. Do you have any built up anger? Do you have unresolved issues? Do you still harbor great pain from a memory? If so, now is the time to heal yourself and find the greatest peace possible, because I believe there is such a thing as "good dementia" and "bad dementia."

People who have not dealt with personal bitterness are more likely to have bad dementia. Resolving bitterness in the midst of dementia would be a difficult task. It's just something to think about.

Anger repressed can poison a relationship as surely as the cruelest words.

—Joyce Brothers

Newfound Memory Resolution

enhanced moments

Spiritual Well-Being

Walk by faith, not by sight.   II Corinthians 5:7

Spirituality is a part of each of our lives. Organized religion provides the expression of our spirituality. For many people with Alzheimer's, organized religion with its beliefs and traditions is an important aspect of their lives – past and present.

Take time to discover the personal religious rituals they have participated in to uphold their beliefs. Reading devotions before going to bed may be a habit of a lifetime for them. Saying prayer before mealtimes may remind them that it is time to eat.

Reading certain Scriptures that they have known since childhood will evoke memories and offer comfort such as the 23rd Psalm, Apostle's Creed, John 3:16, 1 Peter 1:13 and the Lord's Prayer. Displaying significant spiritual symbols in their environment (angels, cross, Mary, Last Supper) may fill a void.

Seeing a picture of Jesus when they open their eyes may bring comfort. Hymns such as "Amazing Grace" and "How Great Thou Art," as well as Sunday school songs such as "Jesus Loves Me" will be known by heart, and singing them will offer comfort to the Alzheimer's person. Even though they may not be able to attend church, many aspects of church may be brought to them.

We did an impromptu stop to see my mother-in-law (with Alzheimer's) this afternoon, so I didn't have her sewing basket with me. I wasn't sure what I was going to do, but I KNEW I wasn't going to start with "How are you?"

So I grabbed her little photo album of her life, and we looked at pictures of her at 13, then 17, then older and married, then with kids. Then I read some scripture to her...showing her where she had underlined certain phrases in her Bible. And then MAGIC! I asked her if she'd like me to sing. She said yes, so I asked her if she knew Amazing Grace. She immediately lit up (the woman who didn't know she'd had any kids, much less what their names were) and started singing, the correct tune and most of the words.

So we sang together, and when we got to the end, I clapped and cheered. And she just BEAMED. It's like it was the first thing she had accomplished well in four years!!!!!

My husband, Pat, said on the way home that he was absolutely amazed!! He never thought there would be that much light in her soul ever again.

—Deb Griffin

Reverend Joseph was a kind gentleman with Alzheimer's disease. When you would talk with him he would lose his words and have difficulty communicating his thoughts. What was wonderful, was that at the end of every activity he was compelled to close in prayer. When he was praying, words would spill out with such feeling and eloquence that we were moved from each experience. It was a blessing to have him with us.

I attended a presentation "Spiritual Well-being and Alzheimer's Disease" given by Ron Kitterman, who is a chaplain of a large care center. He put so eloquently into words what spiritual well-being means to the person with Alzheimer's and how God fits into the picture. His information has become the glue that holds my words together and I would like to summarize and share these thoughts with you.

Spiritual Well-Being

How we understand and value "spirituality" impacts the way we cope with the challenges involved with dementia. A healthy spirit will ease the struggles that you and the person with dementia face, but spirituality is not about faith reversing or curing the disease.

Arthur Freeman suggests that: "[Spiritual] Well-being to some extent has to do with being well, but it has more to do with existing well in the midst of whatever life brings to one. Thus there can be well-being in the midst of suffering." Spiritual well-being is not the same as being well; it is finding meaning in what life presents to us. Finding that meaning brings about healing. The next step is to constantly ask yourself, "What does this person need to enjoy life at the fullest, right now, given the state of his health?" Realize we can still care for a body that has spirit and that is capable of well-being even if it is not capable of being well.

Healing should not be confused with finding a cure. Healing begins with our acceptance of dementia, the changes it brings and by facing the disease head on. Healing comes in many different forms. In the midst of suffering, our loving Creator longs to meet our deepest needs of our heart. God will give us meaning and a sense of well-being in whatever comes our way. When we aspire and strive to walk through the pain, peace will truly deepen and as we receive God's grace we will go to the core of our spiritual journey.

How do we come to terms with what it means to have "Spiritual Well-Being" in our own lives. Our journey can become easier as we discover what it means to have a sense of well-being. When we face our deepest longings, difficult feelings, questions, fears, confusion and pain with dementia and in our own life, this will lead to our awareness of what it means to deepen our spiritual journey. Where does God fit into the world of dementia? In a book called "God Never Forgets" by Don McKim he writes, "God sees the suffering from the inside; God does not look at it from the outside, as through a window. God is internally related to the suffering of the people. God enters fully into the hurtful situation and makes it (God's) own."

Our culture tells us our value is based on what we do and therefore our worth is based on external and not internal things. Regardless of how our culture and others try to dictate to us how to live, we need to try and come to terms with how our Creator sees us. Even though society tells us if we lose autonomy we are no longer human, our value is based in and from God. We are like aluminum pop cans. We start out worth a nickel and when we are done holding the contents, we are still worth a nickel. Again, if we believe we are made in the image of God then we are truly a reflection of God. Our spirituality absolutely impacts us. It is the very essence of our faith. Faith is seeing light with the eyes of our heart, when the eyes of our body see only darkness ahead.

Excerpt from "My Journey into Alzheimer's Disease"

For the past 10 years, I have preached, taught, and studied from the New International Version of the Bible. It became my Bible. Suddenly in my illness, an amazing thing happened. As I struggled to read, I suddenly realized that this version of the Bible did not speak to my heart anymore. I then rummaged through the few books I kept after my retirement and found my old King James Version of the Bible. As I read this old Bible, suddenly the clouds began to lift. My mind somehow went back to the earlier years, and these old words from the King James Version suddenly began to fall in place and to bring new blessings. All my past 10 years with the New International Version have disappeared, and now it is the old King James Version that speaks to me.

As I realized this, I thought of all the older people that I had hoped to comfort by giving them a much more readable New International Version. I now realize my mistake. These modern words did not sound like the Bible to them. As their minds went back in time, they could not identify with these new words. They needed the old Bibles. I also realize now that if a person grew up reading and worshiping in a language other than English, he probably needs a Bible written in the language of his youth for his personal devotions.

God will remember
even if the person with dementia forgets
and the caregiver falls exhausted!

—Ron Kitterman

Newfound Offering Of Spiritual Well-Being

Breaking of Bread

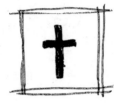

This chapter was written by Teresa Stecker, R.N., who worked for 12 years as a hospice center nurse and is currently a parish nurse. (P.S.—she's Jolene's sister.)

One of the most powerful and common rituals symbolizing Christian faith is communion or the Lord's Supper. Not only is it an outward indication of Christian faith, it is one that is significant since early years of religious training. Communion for Christian believers is an outward expression of worship to indicate their union with Jesus Christ and with His body, the church. It has been described as a love feast with the Savior, the language of our soul.

The Lord Jesus, on the night he was betrayed, took bread, and when he had given thanks, he broke it and said, "This is my body, which is for you; do this in remembrance of me." In the same way, after supper he took the cup, saying, "This cup is the new covenant in my blood; do this, whenever you drink it, in remembrance of me." 1Corinthians 11:23-25 NIV in the Christian Holy Book, the Bible.

Our Protestant church has a nursing home ministry to four care centers including one memory care community. As the Lenten season approached, we rediscovered the significance of communion offered to all believers. Little did we realize the impact of this hour of providing communion to our 80 nursing-home residents. Besides our Christian beliefs about communion, our goal in bringing communion to these residents was to demonstrate that they are needed, honored, indispensable and dignified as members of the body of Christ. (See 1 Corinthians: 12)

We wanted to reach all of their senses. To create the feeling of church, we incorporated several people in the communion including church members, family members, and staff. Even if they did not partake, their presence suggested a church.

We asked church members to dress up in their Sunday best and our pastor to wear his typical attire for a communion service.

We set up a table draped with linen, placed a vase full of roses, and lit candles to create the look and feel of a sanctuary. All the while, hymns were playing in the background. We spent time physically preparing participants such as combing hair, adjusting clothes, and other personal grooming. We prepared each one spiritually through prayer, scripture reading, or conversation regarding the significance of sharing the sacrament of the Lord's Supper. We selected Scripture that has personal significance and familiarity. With communion, we assisted with the receiving of elements. If they were unable to physically drink or eat the bread and wine, we touched the elements to their lips. We prayed individually with each one present and then concluded with corporate recitation of the Lord's Prayer. After the communion, we finished with an act of blessing by giving them a rose, touching their arm, and affirmed their value as a member of the body of Christ.

We also served communion in individual rooms, and it included the same elements of our group communion. The response of the residents was incredible and powerful. It created a solemn and sacred time. In an environment that can be noisy and chaotic, there was an attitude of reverence by all present. After receiving communion, an emotional 80-year-old woman said she had felt the church had forgotten her—until this day. An elderly gentleman wept as we held his hand and prayed for his physical health. A wheelchair-bound person indicated that this was the best day of her life in the care center. As church members, we felt honored and blessed to bring a significant and joyful moment to those individuals with Alzheimer's disease.

We sensed the gratitude of all who participated. This included a wife of an Alzheimer's resident. She indicated that she was in church with her husband for the first time in more than two years. They shared the songs as he remembered the words of a couple of hymns, they shared the act of communion side-by-side, and then they shared the Lord's Prayer as they spoke it together. They had the moment to reconnect with each other, their faith, and their God.

If communion is not happening in your care center, then families need to go the leaders of their church and request provision of communion for their loved ones. Connection with church and its rituals is relevant in creating spiritual well-being. You could be a part of providing this communion service, too.

In my Bible studies, I always bring an object—small seed, fruit cut in half, acorn, hickory nut. Sometimes, I simply have them look at their hands and fingernails— noticing how useful they are. I say, "This is all a part of God's creation." Then I use Genesis 1:11 or Ecclesiastes 3:17. God makes everything beautiful in His time.

When I do the Bible studies this way, they respond and are alert. But if I would preach like I do on Sundays, I lose them.

I also have them feel their hair and ask them, "How many hairs to you suppose you have on your head? God knows. Don't we have a great God?" Then they affirm, "Yes, we have a great God."

When I make it simple, God enters in.

—Chaplain David L. Yoder

When all else fails, simply say, "Let's pray about it."
—Jolene

Newfound Prayer

Find the Blessing

It's understandable as children of people with Alzheimer's that we want our moms back. We want our parents to remember who we are. We go to great lengths to try to restart the part of the brain that has truly died.

We stand with our mom in front of a mirror and say, "Mom, don't you see that I look a lot like you? I am your daughter, Viola." The reply usually goes like this, "You're not my daughter. You are an old lady." If you look deeper into this reply you will realize that she does remember she has children but her children are young. This reiterates the theory that people with Alzheimer's have lost the last 20 to 50 years of their lives.

If we continue to insist that we are their child, a wall may go up, and the parent may be thinking, "Who is this impostor in my room?" Again, we have to be the ones to change, which may mean visiting as a third person. Instead of saying "Mom," use a term of endearment, such as, "Hi Sweetie, or Hey Honey." Or simpler yet, "Hi there. Can I sit next to you to rest my feet?" Then maybe these next stories can become your own.

The mother has Alzheimer's. She has a daughter she has been fighting with for the last 20 years. The daughter only has hurt feelings and carries much anger toward her mother. When the daughter learned more about the disease she realized her mom probably had lost 50 years. The daughter introduced herself by saying, "Hi, Margaret, my name is Judy and I found your photo album. I was hoping you could tell me about the little blond girl in this picture." The mother told the daughter stories about herself she had never heard before. Stories that were filled with love and adoration for this wonderful little girl. The daughter was again reminded of her mother's love and given precious memories to hold that replaced the memories and the anger from the last 20 years. When this mom loses the ability to talk, the daughter can give back the memories she has been given. This was truly a blessing.

Jean's dad, Harold, was always at work when she was growing up. Harold had little time for his family. Harold tended to drink and was physically abusive on occasion when his children were young. Now, Harold has Alzheimer's disease and is living in a care center. When Jean visits, Harold does not recognize her, nor give any indication he knows she is a familiar person to him. However, the staff tells Jean that her father frequently asks if Jean is coming to visit, and when he is displeased, he calls out for Jean to help him. One afternoon, Jean found him staring out the window with a very sad look on his face. "Hi dad. What's wrong?" Jean asked. Harold told her about his little girl, his daughter, and how much he missed her. "I don't think she loves me." Harold said. Jean asked Harold to tell her more about his daughter. What she heard was a tale about a father who did love his daughter, but didn't know how to show it. Harold said, "I just wish I could tell her how much I love her." With tears in her eyes, Jean said, "She knows, dad, she knows." The blessing for Jean was discovering that her dad did love her. He just never knew how to show it.

Some parents may have difficulty showing their love to their own children. It's easier to brag about their children to other people. Grasp the moment and search for the blessings in every situation. You will be surprised at what you find.

A daughter explained to me how she grew up with four brothers and she was the only girl. She and her father had never been very close. After he was diagnosed with Alzheimer's, she became his caregiver. She confided in me that she is getting to know her dad for the first time because he doesn't recognize her.

Look for the blessings as simple as they are. Once you do this, you will find you have more energy to make the changes to enjoy the moments.

> *Rings on my fingers,*
> *Bells on my feet,*
> *I'm Daddy's little girl,*
> *Don't you think I'm sweet.*

Newfound Blessings

enhanced moments

Taking Care of
Yourself

I should have placed this section at the beginning of the book, because you need to take care of yourself before you can take care of someone else. No matter what your situation, start now and get involved with your own life once again. Take time to do the things you love to do, be with people who make you feel good and pamper—no better yet—spoil yourself as often as possible.

Just as we need to relieve stress for a person with dementia, you need to find ways to relieve stress in your own life. It is proven that stress adversely affects brain functioning. Reducing stress helps us function better. Even when you don't feel like it, smile, because just smiling lifts your spirit and relieves stress. Exercising is a great way to relieve stress and increase blood flow to the brain. Meditating 20 minutes in the morning and at night will help you relax.

Of course, eat good foods, lower your fat intake, and drink lots of water (six cups a day). Get lots of rest!!! If the person is having fragmented sleeping patterns and waking up in the middle of the night for a couple of hours, you need to sleep when the person sleeps. This might mean napping at 10:00 in the morning.

Of most importance, take time off from care giving—at least two days a week. I hear many reasons why people feel like they can't take time off. The fact is if you don't take care of yourself first, you will soon be less healthy than the person with dementia. We say the person with Alzheimer's is the victim, but really the one taking care of the person with Alzheimer's is the victim. Sometimes the spouse dies before the person with dementia.

Alzheimer's disease is understandably devastating to families. It creates tension and stress for even the most solid families. It's overwhelming when you are suddenly responsible for finances, the house, and for a person who is dependent on you for the most basic needs (eating, grooming, bathing, dressing). Many times, the best solution is to find a good memory care community.

I strongly recommend you get involved in a support group and connect with someone who has already been through the journey you're embarking on. This group of support people will be able to relate to your frustrations, share the mistakes and solutions, and assure you that what is happening is normal. Seek help from others. It's not an option, it is a necessary step.

> *My brother came to visit me. My husband has Alzheimer's and I was obviously showing frustration, anger and resentment toward my husband. He looked at me and gave me advice that saved my life. "Let someone else take care of him for awhile. Don't wait until your love turns to hate."*
>
> —wife in need

No one should have to lose both of their parents to Alzheimer's. Take care of yourself first.
—Words of Wisdom

Newfound Ways to Reduce Stress

enhanced moments

Helping Hands

Caregivers will need others to get through this time. They are on-call 24-7, in their hearts, if not literally. They feel a deep, personal burden about the needs they fulfill; some were truly called by God to love this way. So lending that helping hand might not be easy—because it will be refused—at first. And yes, the dialog will go something like this:

The caregiver, "No, you don't have to do this."
Your response, "Yes, I want to."
The caregiver, "No, I've never left him before."
Your response, "Just go. We will be fine."
The caregiver, "He might . . . "
Your response, "I said go. You don't have to worry about a thing. I can handle this."
The caregiver, "Well..."
Your response, "We are going to have a good time. You have fun, too."
The caregiver, "Are you sure?"
Your response, "Yes, I'm sure. Take as long as you like."

The caregiver, "I don't know."
Your response, "Well I do. Now scoot." (with a smile)
The caregiver hesitates . . .
Your response, "I said scoot and enjoy yourself."

Once the caregiver experiences that it is OK for someone else to help her, she will be quicker to accept help the next time. The first time is the most difficult.

The neighborhood, church, and community can be the saving grace for a person taking care of someone with Alzheimer's or dementia. Even though they may not ask for help they will need others to get through this time in their life.

The important part is for someone to set up a schedule to spread out the help. When we visit or help all at once we are actually adding more stress to the care provider. We, in a team effort, can make a huge difference.

How to give a helping hand

- Do their laundry
- Schedule people to drop off food every other day.
- Mow their lawn (Don't ask them, just do it.)
- Ask if there is anything you can get for them when you go to the grocery store
- Take the person with dementia on a country drive or to a ball game, so the care provider can take a break
- Offer to stay with the person with dementia so the care provider can run errands, get their hair done, visit a friend
- Give them meals that can be put in the freezer and then easily cooked in the oven
- Mail them movie tickets or restaurant certificates anonymously
- Clean their house and do the dishes

- Share your garden vegetables
- Take care of their loved one so they can have a night off

A good way to help with laundry or cleaning inside the house is to find out when they will be out of the house so they don't have to watch you help. It's too easy for them to feel guilty when we help while they are watching.

People will have difficulty accepting help and will probably refuse initially, but keep persisting. Whenever possible help anonymously. When offering help, reassure and say, "You are my friend. I care about you, so please let me help."

When we truly care for ourselves, it becomes possible to care far more profoundly about other people. The more alert and sensitive we are to our own needs, the more loving and generous we can be toward others.
—Eda LeShan

Newfound Ways To Accept Help from Others

enhanced moments

Final Moments

This chapter was written by Teresa Stecker, R.N., who worked for 12 years as a hospice center nurse. She now works as a parish nurse for First Church of the Nazarene in Iowa City, Iowa.

As with all of us, there comes a time when the journey of life comes to an end for the person with Alzheimer's. These final days may go quickly or move slowly. They may be with or without signs of discomfort. As caregivers, we can bring comfort by advocating for the person to be as free of pain and as comfortable as possible. This can be assisted by talking to your physician and/or care facility to refer end of life care to the local hospice organization. They specialize in providing comfort to the dying and support to the caregivers. This can be done in the home or in a facility.

As an individual moves to within hours of death, signs that may be present include: restlessness, slower and more irregular breathing, congestion, cold hands and feet, and eyes open. After a few gasping breaths, the journey of life on this earth is complete.

Being sensitive to family needs at this time may include privacy, quiet, being willing to listen, washing of the body, significant touch, prayer, calling a religious leader, putting a specific clothes on the body, positioning the body as directed by family, and arranging for others to visit prior to the arrival of the mortician. Let family members guide your response. However family reacts, the significant thing is to be available, be accepting of them, their wishes and their grief expression.

It is beneficial to your family and yourself to formally communicate your wishes regarding your medical treatment at the end of life. It is best for this to be done while you are in good health mentally and physically. These plans should be expressed verbally to your family but also should be written in a living will and a durable power of attorney document. Check with your physician or lawyer regarding these documents.

As I looked at this title, I wondered how I could convey the final moments of joy I have witnessed as a hospice nurse. For us, death is viewed as defeat or the end. It is hidden and not talked about but it something we all will face. Let me tell you what I have seen in the final moments of joy while walking through end-of-life journey with many individuals with Alzheimer's and their families.

I've seen the positive affect of an individual's approaching death makes others stop and consider their lives. I've seen reconciliation in families. I've seen forgiveness offered where it was denied for several years. I've seen families huddle together in unity, overcoming years of bitter isolation. I've seen laughter ring out over a family joke in the midst of tears. I've seen quiet smiles of remembrance of a mother's last embrace in the midst of sadness. I've seen loyalty and perseverance, where so many times they just wanted to run away.

Sometimes it has been the struggle of feeling like we could have done more or the sense of failure in that relationship. But in thoughtful recollection, we realize we did our best and are only human.

For as we have sought to bring moments of joy to others, it returns. Our own moments of joy come as we rest, remember, and sense the feeling that we did all we knew how to do within our human capacity to show love. It is our greatest gift and it is the gift that no one can take from us. May you be gentle and loving with yourself as you reflect on the moments of joy you brought to lives that will only repay you in memories and in your inner sense of peace. May that be your moment of joy!

> *A caregiver dressed up as an angel one year for Halloween. She walked into this lady's room and the lady asked, "Are you here to take me home?" Well of course she didn't know what to do so she left the room and went to talk with the administrator. The administrator said, "Go in there and hold her hand and walk with her." So she did. She went back to her room, held her hand and said, "It is time to go home. I will walk with you. It's OK." The lady died within 5 minutes.*

It's OK to go home. It shouldn't be a bad thing to go home. I think the important point here is that no one wants to go alone. We need to make it OK and we need to walk with them.

You matter to the last moment of your life, and we will do all we that we can, not only to help you die peacefully, but to live until you die.
—Dame Cicely Saunders, Founder of the Hospice Movement, London, 1968

Conclusion

Caregivers, you give and you give and you give all day long. Be sure to give to yourself first, then give to the people you love most, your spouse and kids. Then give to the person or persons with dementia. If you put your work (caregiving) number one in your life you may just lose the other people in your life because you have nothing left to give.

Say, "I have worked too long, I am going home." No one is going to give you permission to fit joy into your schedule. No one is going to give you permission to go home. Your boss is going to say, "Can you do another shift?" You are the only person who can give yourself permission to do the things that create joy in your life. When you have joy in your life you are able to give joy away.

You have gained many new ideas and it can be a bit overwhelming. Simply choose the ones that you are excited about tackling and practice, practice, practice. When you have it down pat, come back to the book, and pick another area you want to work on. Small successes supply the beginning to a better day.

Accept that you can only change yourself. You cannot make anyone else do what you want them to do. Be a role model and let them visually see that your actions are creating better reactions in the person with Alzheimer's. As the old saying goes—actions speak louder than words. True.

I sometimes make this journey sound like butterflies and cupcakes. That cannot be further from the true suffering and pain that is caused by Alzheimer's. But you are on this road, so you must get to your destination as safely as possible. Watch for the signs to give yourself some direction, pull off the road, take a cat nap whenever necessary, and accept help from others when something breaks down. In fact, take a couple of friends with you so they can drive when you get worn out. And last but not least, savor the moments of joy.

On our 57th wedding anniversary we ate our lunch together. My wife remarked that we did not have children. Then she said, "We have been married for a long time and that has given me more time to love you." I laughed and time stood still for me to catch my breath. It may be awhile before I experience such a "moment of joy".

—Don Alexander, husband and caregiver

Look beyond the wall of this disease and focus on the person who needs you. Love and care with a genuine heart. That's when you will fly, feel warmth, and start smelling the daisies.

—*Jolene Brackey*

I want to thank you, Lord,
for being close to me so far this day.

With your help I haven't been impatient, lost my temper,
been grumpy, judgmental, or envious of anyone.

BUT
I will be getting out of bed in a minute, and I think
I will really need your help then!
Amen

enhanced moments

.

Create a Moment....

Sneak the chocolate in your pocket ~ recite their favorite poem ~ laugh along ~ bite into fresh strawberries ~ whistle a tune ~ talk about "goin fishin" ~ ice cream, ice cream, ice cream, ~ go for a walk ~ bring a jar of pickles ~ seek shade ~ turn off the TV ~ dance ~ watch the birds ~ picnic in a park ~ bring fried chicken ~ re-read the classics ~ play the piano ~ sing out loud ~ hold hands ~ talk to them even if they don't talk back ~ smile a lot ~ catch a firefly ~ talk over an old fishing lure ~ drink lemonade together ~ buy their favorite music ~ bring a cheeseburger ~ help them write a letter ~ send mail ~ share a funny story ~ send a simple surprise package (just to open) ~ rub lotion into their hands ~ look them in the eye ~ stroke their hair ~ hug them until they let go ~ remember the good times ~ sing them to sleep ~ notice the clouds ~ pick their favorite flower ~ watch a sunset ~ let them watch you fly a kite ~ hold a baby ~ or hold a doll ~ visit outside in the breeze ~ snap beans ~ notice them ~ listen to their stories ~ sit in the sun ~ say yes A LOT ~ be more than a daughter, just be their friend ~ spray their favorite perfume ~ stay with them when they are afraid ~ reassure that you have taken care of everything ~ be relaxed ~ tell them how terrific they are ~ cover their lap with a warm afghan ~ let them take along that worn ugly orange recliner ~ share warm homemade bread with butter ~ provide a big comfy couch to nap on ~ let them wear their favorite outfit day after day ~ compliment them (on that outfit) ~ watch a puppy play ~ come to them with a joke

~ sing a fond hymn over and over ~ learn what they have to teach ~ use your ears more than your mouth ~ wave and smile when you part ~ ask for their opinion ~ nibble on a gooey cinnamon roll ~ let them be right ~ ask them to help you ~ thank them for helping you the best way they know how ~ be flexible ~ include them in conversations ~ accept them as they are ~ become their advocate ~ make them comfortable ~ touch, feel, talk about their treasured possessions ~ look at old photos ~ share a secret ~ do what they like to do ~ eat a Sunday dinner 3 times a week ~ let them have, let them be, let them do whatever brings comfort and assurance ~ love them no matter what

....Isn't that what you would want?

BIBLIOGRAPHY

Freeman, Arthur. "Spirituality, Well-being, and Ministry." JPC Vol. 52, No. 1, Spring 1998: page 7.

Johnson, Barbara. Boomerang Joy: Joy That Goes Around, Comes Around. Zondervan Publishing House 1998.

Jones, Moyra. Gentlecare: Changing the Experience of Alzheimer's Disease In a Positive Way. Moyra Jones Resources 1996.

Kitterman, Ron. "Spiritual Well-being and Alzheimer's Disease" 1998

McKim, Donald K. God Never Forgets: Faith, Hope, and Alzheimer's Disease. Ed. Westminister John. Louisville, KN: Knox Press, 1997.

Nelson, Dawn. "Massaging Victims of Alzheimer's Disease: Communication and Caring Through Touch." Massage No. 53, Jan/Feb 1995: page 24-29

Moments of Discomfort was written by Lori Linton Nelson, RN, MN, PMHNP. She is a Psychiatric Mental Health Nurse Practitioner and Clinical Research Fellow at the Benedictine Institute For Long Term Care in Mt. Angel, Oregon. She is working on a grant through the Hartford Institute on Geriatric Nursing at New York University to improve pain management delivery in the elderly population.

Spread the Holidays Throughout the Year, and Intimacy were written by Jeanne Yordi.

McGowin, Diana Friel. Living in the Labyrinth: A personal journey through the maze of Alzheimer's. Delacorte Press, 1993

Davis, Robert. My Journey into Alzheimer's Disease Tyndale House Publishers Inc., 1989

Strauss, Claudia J. Talking to Alzheimer's: Simple Ways to Connect When You Visit with a Family Member or Friend New Harbinger Publications, Inc 2001

McCone, Virginia. Butterscotch Sundaes: My Mom's Story of Alzheimer's Autumn Sparrow Press, 2003

Gray, David D. I Want to Remember: A Son's Reflection on His Mother's Alzheimer Journey. Roundtable Press, 1993

About the Author

Jolene Brackey began her career as an interior designer after graduating from Iowa State University. But she soon realized that she derived great joy from helping people improve the interiors of their lives, rather than their homes. When she left her interior design job, the first job available was in an Alzheimer' special care unit as an activity director. She didn't know what Alzheimer's was but she knew she liked older people. Before long, she realized that God had given her a gift. She found ways to create positive outcomes and moments of joy for the individuals with the disease, their loved ones, and professional caregivers.

Eager to share her practical solutions and insights, Jolene began speaking at educational seminars. Her message of hope, encouragement—along with generous helpings of humor—was warmly embraced by family members and professional caregivers alike. So, she established a business, Enhanced Moments, to help guide people through the Alzheimer's journey.

Jolene found affirmation of her calling in many ways, including this story:

Two years after I started my business, my mom found a heart I made in Sunday school when I was 7. On the heart I wrote: "Love is . . . knowing Jesus, helping Mom and Dad, helping make the bed, and helping old people."

God has planted this gift and prepared me for this journey. I encourage all people, young and old, to discover your gift and use it to make a difference in the lives of others.

If you are interested in having Jolene Brackey speak to your organization or would like additional training material, please contact:

Enhanced Moments
P.O. Box 326
Polson, Montana 59860
email: jolene@enhancedmoments.com
www.enhancedmoments.com